REAL
MOSQUITOES
Don't Eat Meat

REAL MOSQUITOES
Don't Eat Meat

THIS AND OTHER INQUIRIES INTO THE ODDITIES OF NATURE

BRAD WETZLER

Outside
BOOKS

W. W. Norton & Company, Inc.
New York • London

The present work appeared in a slightly different version in *Outside* Magazine.

ISBN 0-393-06157-4

Library of Congress Cataloging-in-Publication Data has been applied for.

Cover photo © Theo Allofs
Interior illustration by Jason Schneider, Sex Puppy Studio
Book design and composition by Dawn DeVries Sokol

W. W. Norton & Company, Inc., 500 Fifth Avenue, New York, NY 10110
www.wwnorton.com

W. W. Norton & Company Ltd., Castle House, 75/76 Wells Street, London
W1T 3QT

10 9 8 7 6 5 4 3 2 1

Contents

Acknowledgments

There are a number of people who deserve special notice:
Kermit Hummel, the fine editor at W.W. Norton's
Countryman Press who made sure the quality of this book
was as good as the column itself; Larry Burke, *Outside*'s
illustrious founder; editor Hal Espen, who oversees the
column every month and assures that it's up to standards;
the column editors from 2001 to the present, Eric Hansen,
Chris Keyes, and my most recent cohort, Will Palmer, whose
loyal behind-the-scenes toiling made the trains run on time
and shaped the column into the "Wild Thing" of beauty
that it was each month; Alex Heard and Katie Arnold, for
top-editing my work; and, of course, *Outside*'s Stephanie
Pearson, who fielded a number of queries in this volume.
I also wish to thank Jason Holley, for his weird and wonder-
ful illustrations during the past four years; and the hardest
working group of all, *Outside*'s ever-evolving staff of edito-
rial interns and assistant editors, who did the lion's share of
the fact checking: Claire Antoszewski, Sam Bass, Ki Bassett,
Misty Blakesley, John Bradley, Ryan Brandt, Josh Brockman,
Josh Calhoun, Emily Crawford, Christine Cyr, Christian
DeBenedetti, Carol Greenhouse, Michael Hoyer, Catharine
Livingston, Megan Miller, Dina Mishev, Christian Nardi,
Sally Schumaier, Katie Showalter, Kate Siber, Tim Sohn,
Jason Stevenson, Dan Strumpf, Jesse Sunenblick, Pieter van
Noordennen, Jennifer Villeneuve, Jonathan Waldman,
Cameron Walker, David Weissman, and Lindsay Yaw.

Introduction

"If I had only known, I would have been a locksmith," said Albert Einstein, speaking about the atomic bomb. At "The Wild File," *Outside* magazine's clearinghouse for all crazy questions on nature and the wild life, the implications of our work are far less dire than the ones faced by the father of relativity, but somehow the feeling is the same. For the author of this column, there are times when opening up an envelope from one of our readers is to open a can of worms. It's not your fault, dear reader: You were just curious. But here at our home offices in Santa Fe, New Mexico—about four hours north of the Trinity Site, as fate would have it—unlocking the secrets of Mother Nature can mean entering a world of mind-boggling logarithms, ever-deepening mystery, and the occasional toxic-waste cleanup.

Fortunately, as it celebrates its tenth year in the always thrilling pages of *Outside,* the Wild File has never been more popular. The Class V torrent of questions we receive each month is evidence of that. Your tales of mad dashes to the mailbox to claw open the clear plastic wrapper and flip to that special page are evidence of that. We hear from families with kids who use the Wild File as a basis for science projects that go on to win awards, thus helping to push the blocking sled of scientific knowledge even farther down the field. But the best evidence is the book you're reading, which represents the best work of yours truly and my predecessor Stephanie Pearson, who has contributed twelve articles to this book.

Why do people love the Wild File? For the same reason that jumping off a rope swing into a cool pond on a hot summer day is enjoyable: It's fun! As Hampton Sides, the column's creator and the editor of *Why Moths Hate Thomas Edison,* the first Wild File collection, mentioned in that book, the column appeals to the prying little rug rat in all of us, to that spark of curiosity and feeling of awe in everything that shaped our entire being as children.

If fun is one of our top priorities, then the other one is getting it right. We take our jobs seriously, which is why every month sees a flurry of e-mails, phone calls, drafts, and an epic struggle of Researchers vs. the Elusive Truth. First we have to decide on a good mix of questions—sometimes a mini–Manhattan Project in itself—then the process gets under way in our downtown office, the Adobe Palace, where we implore the gods of trivia and humor to guide us safely down the road of accuracy and outstanding yuks. I retreat to my satellite office—a small adobe house a few miles away, out near the Wal-Mart—and start calling up dozens of scientists, trying to find the one man or woman who specializes in the topic at hand—and, hopefully, speaks English. Next, the editors, just itching to get their hands on my work and rip it to shreds, get together with the daunt-less fact-checkers, whip up some strong herbal tea, and roll up their sleeves. More pestering calls are made to our expert authority—who by this point has likely mysteriously disap-peared on "sabbatical"—plus half a dozen other pros, to ensure that I heard right and that the scientist we're quoting is not the one renegade who believes he can turn 1,200 years of scientific knowledge on its head. The folks at HQ keep doing their thing (editors: can't live with 'em, can't stuff 'em deep into the earth in natural salt caverns like so much radioactive waste) and, once our illustrator has made the page look as good as it sounds, we release it to the printing press and the world at large. Finally, we all head over to the bar for a round of something a little stiffer than herbal tea. Yeah, life could be worse.

Sometimes the hardest part of answering your questions is trying to figure out where to begin. Take the time someone wanted to know—for whatever twisted reason—whether there are any animals capable of killing people without actually making contact. It's not the kind of information scientists have readily available in spreadsheet form. So we started asking ourselves: What if you were in a swimming pool and a rat bit through some nearby electrical circuits, then fell in with the sparking cable still in its teeth? How about if an eagle dropped a rock on your head, mistaking you for—I don't know—an overgrown field mouse? In the end, we determined that other scenarios might be more plausible and, in one case, actually documented—namely, the eleventh-hour discovery that some unhinged monkeys once offed two humans by dropping coconuts on their heads.

Other times, a question that we think will be a slam dunk turns into a nightmare. Like the time a reader asked what ski area lies closest to the equator. Before we knew it, secondary and tertiary questions crept in to complicate matters: What's the definition of a ski area? Does the qualifying place need to have a chairlift, or does a decades-old rope tow, from which the rope is sometimes stolen, count? If the rope tow is out of order this month but rumored to be back up by next winter, does that count? Proprietors of tropical ski areas aren't easy to find, but soon enough our dedicated, multilingual interns were on the phone with the one Ecuadorian ski bum we could track down who was acquainted with the rickety old place. Because we always triangulate our sources to be certain we're correct, we eventually got confirmation, but not before running up one monster of a phone bill.

Yet we keep at it, and it's your curiosity that keeps firing us up to dive into that cool pond with you. Your questions are our bread and butter—it may take a village to raise a kid, but it takes 650,000 subscribers and all their endless idiosyncratic ponderings to supply fresh, original questions. Choosing which ones to leave out can be painful; sometimes, not so much. For example:

Are islands "hooked" to anything under the water? If not, why don't they float around?

Can you name the only animal with four knees?

It is common knowledge that warm air rises and cold air sinks—is that the reason that the South Pole is colder than the North Pole?

Why do old men fart so much?

Why is there so much attention, on television and in hunting magazines, on hunters who take pride in "bagging" a trophy deer with guns, arrows, calls, etc.? Those macho hunters out there should try hunting hog with a dog and knife: the ultimate man-pride sport.

For better or worse, the Wild File simply couldn't exist without its readers. Not just because you give us your questions and offer your feedback about what we got right and what we didn't get quite right. It's more the intangibles, the buzz you create when you tell your co-workers about "some crazy question I saw in that outdoors magazine" and quiz them on how much Mount Everest weighs. You, the Wild File reader—the conduit for releasing our weird, deluded research into the world—make the final contribution to humanity's understanding of the world. Just don't ask us what that contribution is.

Keep watching for the Wild File every month, and we'll keep working to give you a variety of quirky subjects, and to do it in an accurate, surprising, and friendly way, so it's ready to be wadded up, stuffed in the pocket of your poncho, taken on a forced march led by your friend Rufus, and read by flashlight in the tent. Should you come away from your next jaunt into the mysterious beyond with fresh questions, we'll be waiting for you. Send them to *Outside,* 400 Market Street, Santa Fe, New Mexico 87501, or wildfile@ outsidemag.com, or submit them via Outside Online at www.outsideonline.com/wildfile.

Brad Wetzler
Santa Fe, New Mexico

Chapter 1

THE GREAT Beyond

METEOROLOGY, ASTRONOMY, AND THE MOON

Q: How accurately north is the North Star? Who first noted its northness?

—*MICHAEL DUNN, NASHUA, NEW HAMPSHIRE*

A: Polaris, which is known to modern-day earthlings as the North Star, is off true north by only 0.75 degree. But it hasn't always been the North Star. That's because the Earth, experiencing the gravitational tug of the sun and the moon, wobbles a little like a Weeble on its axis of rotation. If you extended the Earth's axis into space, the wobbling would cause the axis to draw a circle at the opposite end of the sky, with a diameter of about 47 degrees, once every 26,000 years. So while our planet's northern axis currently points toward Polaris, if you rewind or fast-forward 13,000 years, it will point to another major star, Vega. (By contrast, the sky above our southern axis is devoid of bright objects, which is why there is no South Star.) As for someone "discovering" the North Star, according to Bruce Koehn, a research scientist at Arizona's Lowell Observatory, "that's like saying someone discovered that the sky is blue." Whichever North Star you're referring to, says Koehn, "people have almost certainly used it for navigation since prehistory."

Why are all the planets round? Since space is a vacuum, there should be no resistance, and therefore no friction to cause the rounding.

—BOB DETMERS, HAMILTON, MONTANA

A: You're correct; friction doesn't shape the planets. Rather, it's gravity that dictates their spherical figure. A planet has so much matter that its total gravitational force acts as though it emanates from the center, pulling the outside particles toward the massive core. And when everything on the outside is being pulled inward with identical force, a sphere is the only possible shape it can assume. Furthermore, the more massive the planet, the stronger its force of gravity. "On really big planets, the force is so strong that tall mountains would be flattened," says Myles Standish, an astronomer at NASA's Jet Propulsion Lab in Pasadena, California, "but on smaller planets, the force isn't as great, so very strong structures wouldn't crumble." Knowing that, you can bet that alpinists of the future will have their sights set on smaller planets like Mars, where the volcano Olympus Mons rises over 80,000 feet, more than twice the height of Mount Everest.

METEOROLOGY, ASTRONOMY, AND THE MOON

Q: What exactly is cloud seeding, and why isn't anyone doing it in the drought-plagued West?

—*JOE BAUMGARDNER, EVERGREEN, COLORADO*

A: The Hopi have long danced with snakes to petition the forces of nature for rain, but for the past 50 years conjurers have released silver iodide into clouds from planes or ground-based generators. Sounds like sci-fi, but cloud seeding is based on sound principles. Because rain and snow are formed by water condensing around particles of dust and ice, it follows that adding particles to the air will encourage more rain and snow to form. And so it does—we think. As Brooks Martner, a research meteorologist for the National Oceanic and Atmospheric Administration (NOAA) in Boulder, Colorado, explains, "experiments have indisputably shown that seeding produces billions of ice crystals in supercooled clouds. But the evidence is less convincing that these crystals grow large enough to fall out of the cloud." The American Meteorological Society has acknowledged that the practice seems to work, and the private companies that work in the $4-million-a-year industry couldn't agree more. This past winter, a Colorado outfit was paid $650,000 to boost snowfall around the Denver area. There was a 20 percent increase over the previous five years, with totals that doubled those of the year before. But was all—or any—of that snow the result of cloud seeding? It's an unknown, and one that's further complicated in times of drought, when there aren't enough good clouds around to seed. Bottom line, there should always be room for a few talented rain dancers.

Q: How much does the Earth weigh? Does anybody know?

—DEBORAH HARDT, MCGREW, NEBRASKA

A: Technically, the Earth weighs nothing, thanks to that old scientific chestnut that defines weight as a measure of the Earth's gravitational pull on another mass. The real question is: How strongly is the Earth and its terrestrial matter attracted to itself—or, more simply put, what is the Earth's own mass? The answer is incomprehensibly huge and impressive enough to toss out with great effect at cocktail parties: 5,972 sextillion metric tons. In pounds, that would be 13,160 followed by 21 zeros. The figure only came to light a year ago as a bonus factoid while Jens Gundlach, a University of Washington professor of physics, was busy solving a different mathematical conundrum altogether: finding the precise value of the 300-year-old unknown called Newton's Gravitational Constant. How'd he do it? The calculations are about as unfathomable as the figure itself, so let's just say he used gold-plated Pyrex dishes, stainless-steel balls, a host of microcomputers, a pen, a notepad, and a cranium full of brains. "The last equation took about ten seconds," boasts Gundlach. "I just did it on a piece of paper." OK, next time how about the weight of the atmosphere? *(Contributed by Stephanie Pearson)*

Q: If I'm riding my bike during a lightning storm, will the tires keep me grounded?

—CHUCK PENGILLY, FAIRBANKS, ALASKA

A: That's a negative. While it's true that rubber is a good insulator, a half-inch or so of tread is simply not enough to keep a bolt of lightning carrying tens of millions of volts from obliterating you in its effort to reach the ground. "Think of it like this," says Paul Krehbiel, a physics professor at the New Mexico Institute of Mining and Technology, who has had many close calls studying electrical storms. "Air is a superb insulator, too, so if a lightning bolt traveling at 75 miles per second makes it through 2 or 3 miles of atmosphere, a measly old tire is unlikely to offer much help." That also goes for your car, which protects you only because its steel cage diverts any electrical charge into the ground. So what's a poor biker who gets caught in a storm to do? The National Lightning Safety Institute advises that you ditch your bike, stay away from trees, water, and metal objects, adopt a low crouching position, and cover your ears.

Q: What makes the moon look bigger at moonrise?

—*Philip D. Armour III, Kaneohe, Hawaii*

A: You've hit on a curiosity that has stumped many lofty thinkers, and probably most of the hot dates you've ever moon-gazed with. It's called the moon illusion, and it's just that: a trick on your eyes and brain. Most viewers perceive the full moon on the horizon to be 50 to 75 percent larger than it is at its zenith, but the orb is the same distance from Earth at both points. Scientists have hundreds of explanations, with many still clinging to a notion Aristotle put forth around 350 B.C.: that the image of the horizon moon is magnified by our lenslike atmosphere. But a father-son team, retired New York University psychology professor Lloyd Kaufman and IBM physicist James H. Kaufman, did a series of experiments in 1999 that they say confirm the "apparent distance" theory, suggested by Ptolemy in the second century and formulated by Arab physicist al-Hasan nine hundred years later. It involves the brain's distance-gauging mechanism, which constantly adjusts to make the images we view jibe with the reality we know is there; the brain can't make these "rescalings" without using an object's surroundings as a guide. When you see the horizon moon, your mind takes into account the terrain in front of it and concludes that it's really far away and, therefore, really big. When the moon's overhead, the cues are gone, and the visual center in your brain is unable to assess its distance (it's 249,000 miles away, after all) and thus can't determine its size. Neurophysicists are working to prove this once and for all, but for now, score one for the Ptolemeister.

How many feet would the oceans need to rise to cause a globally catastrophic event?

—*JIM CONCKLIN, CHICAGO, ILLINOIS*

A: It all hinges on your definition of "catastrophic"—and which hotly contested estimates you choose to believe. Global warming is, after all, one of the world's most feverishly debated issues, so predictions range widely. According to Environmental Protection Agency figures, U.S. coast levels could jump 1 foot over the next century, which could permanently alter fragile marine estuary ecosystems, like the Chesapeake Bay, and potentially deluge the Mississippi River's floodplain. Not catastrophic enough? Consider a surge of roughly 3 feet, the upper estimate that the United Nations predicts by 2100 if the global-warming trend continues. It would ruin 16 percent of Bangladesh's rice production, destroy 12 percent of Egypt's agricultural land, displace 72 million Chinese, and partially sink major low-lying areas, like the Mekong Delta. Too apocalyptic? Well, if you're envisioning the ocean-covered Earth shown in Kevin Costner's 1995 flop, *Waterworld*, don't worry: There's not enough H_2O on Earth, including what's in the polar ice caps, to cover even half of the planet's dry land.

Q: When I camp out in the desert, why are fewer stars visible at 4 a.m. than at midnight?

—BRADLEY SMITH, LOS ANGELES, CALIFORNIA

A: Even though the sky might look pitch-black at both times, more stars are obscured in the early morning because that nether time we call twilight actually begins as early as two hours before sunrise (and endures up to two hours past sunset). According to astronomer Jeff Chester, of the U.S. Naval Observatory, in Washington, D.C., there are three distinct phases of twilight. In the morning, the first phase is astronomical twilight; if you were in Palm Springs on the summer solstice, it would arrive at 3:52 A.M., and you would start to see fewer stars than you had an hour earlier. After that, at 4:31, would come nautical twilight (when the user of a sextant can see both the horizon and the major stars) and, at 5:07, civil twilight (when it's light enough for people to do "normal outdoor activities" without artificial light). Civil twilight is the indigo phase that most of us know as twilight, and only a few stars would still be visible, fading out until the sun first appeared, at 5:36 A.M.

METEOROLOGY, ASTRONOMY, AND THE MOON

Q: If lightning strikes the water while I'm scuba diving, how far away do I need to be to avoid getting hit?

—CHRIS WOJCIK, POINT PLEASANT, NEW JERSEY

A: Since mineral-laced H$_2$O is a shockingly good conductor of electricity, it's wise to stay completely dry during an electrical storm. But if circumstances demand otherwise, you're better off scuba diving than, say, swimming, boating, or practicing your belly flop off the high dive. According to a law of physics commonly known as the skin effect, most of the electricity in lightning travels on the surface of an object—be it a copper wire, a metal mast, or a bay off the coast of Belize—as opposed to within it. Some of the lightning's zap will penetrate the water, perhaps 10 feet directly below the strike, but otherwise the charge spreads out along the surface, dissipating by various degrees (depending on things like salinity and pollution levels) as it radiates from the point of contact. Since it takes only a few amps to fry a human's circuits and a bolt of lightning is about 25,000 amps, snorkelers and swimmers need to be at least 1,500 feet away from the point of impact to have a decent shot at survival. Scuba divers, as long as they're not surfacing at the strike zone, will be spared entirely.

. . . .

Q: What's the origin of the term "horse latitudes"?

—LEWIS LANSFORD, DURHAM, ENGLAND

A: Not to be confused with the doldrums (they're near the equator), the horse latitudes are two bands of high pressure—at roughly 30 to 35 degrees north and south—known for their maddeningly light, fitful winds. The *Oxford English Dictionary* calls the genesis of the term "uncertain," but many experts think it was inspired by the name Spanish mariners gave to the waters southwest of their country: *El Golfo de las Yeguas*, "the Mares' Sea," possibly a nod to the capriciousness of those animals. The first known use of the term was by a G. Forrester, who in 1777 wrote that the area was "fatal to horses and other cattle" en route to the Americas. Why? To lighten loads or save water, the thinking goes, crews would toss horses overboard. Take your pick, but if you go sailing there, bring a motor—with plenty of horsepower.

Q: What are snow cups?

—*TAMMY LUNDQUIST, SOUTH LAKE TAHOE, CALIFORNIA*

A: Better known as sun cups or, technically, ablation hollows, these dimplelike depressions form on snowfields that have been exposed to prolonged intense sunlight. According to Meredith Betterton, an applied-mathematics professor at the University of Colorado who has modeled them extensively, Americans are most likely to find them in the Rockies and the Sierra, where the high-altitude sun is brightest. As light hits any small dip in the snow's surface, it bounces off the sides, causing the bottom to melt fastest and creating a rapidly deepening trough. Sun cups are a mild nuisance, but since they rarely grow bigger than 6 inches across, they don't really hinder climbers or skiers. The same can't be said for a related phenomenon called penitentes. Mostly found high in the Andes, these occur when dips in the snow melt down so far that they leave columns of ice up to 30 feet tall. Named for their resemblance to praying monks, penitentes form only in very dry conditions, causing them to be hard as rock—"an ice climber's dream," says mountaineer Todd Burleson, who has encountered massive penitentes on Everest's north side. "But the smaller ones," he says, "are a nightmare. To pass through them, you have to smack them with your ice ax and kick them out of the way." Now is that any way to treat a monk?

Q: Is it ever too cold to snow?

—*PETER HAGGART, MOSCOW, IDAHO*

A: It's a popular misconception that it can be too cold to snow. According to Andy Heymsfield, senior scientist at the National Center for Atmospheric Research, in Boulder, Colorado, the key to getting snow in extreme cold lies in humidity. As long as the temperature is at or below 32 degrees Fahrenheit and the humidity is above 60 percent, says Heymsfield, then ice crystals—tiny dustlike motes of snow—will form inside the clouds and may be pulled to earth by gravity. How can there be humidity (i.e., liquid water suspended in the atmosphere) below the freezing point? Generally speaking, ice crystals form on tiny pieces of dust called ice nuclei. These nuclei lend a structure on which the water can crystallize. However, there are often not enough ice nuclei to go around inside the cloud, in which case the water remains in a liquid state—and can even become supercooled, reaching minus 40 degrees or below. When these supercooled droplets bump up against an existing microscopic ice crystal, the water attaches and finally freezes, forming the large and elaborate crystals we call snowflakes. Is it true that no two snowflakes are alike? Yes and no. But that's a whole other ball of, ahem, snow.

Real Mosquitoes

Q: I was reading *The Grapes of Wrath* recently, and I was wondering, are we likely to see another Dust Bowl soon?
—*DAVE COX, BOULDER, COLORADO*

A: As any transplanted Okie will tell you, one Dust Bowl is plenty for a lifetime. While experts warn us not to be surprised if we see another catastrophic drought like the one that scoured the Great Plains during the 1930s, they also say it's not likely we'll experience the sky-obscuring "black blizzards" that blotted out the sun for days at a time. "If you look at long-term records, decade-long droughts happen twice every 100 years," says Donald Wilhite, director of the National Drought Mitigation Center, in Lincoln, Nebraska. But unlike farmers of the thirties—who believed that tilling soil would release moisture that would then fall as rain—today's farmers attempt to reduce the exposure of valuable topsoil to the wind, a battle fought by agriculturists worldwide. So while we may not experience Dust Bowl Redux, much of the nation is already a few years into what could become a catastrophic drought. This dry spell, says Wilhite, could be especially damaging to the millions of people who have migrated to southwestern cities, where water supplies are dubious. Our advice: Forget about migrating to California, and stock up on Evian while you still can.

Q: Is there a magnetic pull in space? If so, in what direction would a compass point?

—*Levi Strong, Caldwell, Kansas*

A: Don't blame space junk, but yes, there is magnetism in space. Magnetic fields, which are produced by the dynamo effect caused by spinning liquid iron, such as the core of a planet, are found throughout the universe. "The Earth's magnetic field extends to a specific boundary called the magnetosphere," explains Jeffrey Love, a geo-magnetism scientist with the U.S. Geological Survey. Once you leave our magnetic field, you come under the sway of the sun's magnetic force, called the Interplanetary Magnetic Field. But here your compass might be off by as

METEOROLOGY, ASTRONOMY, AND THE MOON

many as 40 degrees, since the solar wind—streams of ion-ized gas particles—constantly "blows" the sun's magnetic field in several directions. Unlike the straight lines pro-duced by the Earth's magnetic field, Love says, the sun's lines of force "resemble a tangled plate of spaghetti." As you moved out into interstellar space, you'd find several sources of magnetism—the spiral arms of the Milky Way, enormous clouds of dust and gas, black holes, super-novas—any of which might influence a compass's read-ing. So when you bid on that spaceship of the future on eBay, make sure it has a guidance system of the future. A compass won't do you much good out there—and forget about a GPS.

●　　●　　●　　●　　●　　●　　●　　●

Q Can earthquakes harm fish and marine mammals?

—JACKIE ROHRER, MONTREAL, QUEBEC, CANADA

A: About 80 percent of earthquakes occur in oceans, mostly along the seismically volatile Pacific Rim. For sea critters, the worst thing they're likely to suffer is an earache. Brandon Southall, a marine biologist for the National Oceanic and Atmospheric Administration, says quakes cre-ate some of the loudest natural noises in the ocean, in the form of ultra-low-frequency rumbles that large whales can hear from thousands of miles away. Scientists don't know whether this causes pain, but confused cetaceans have been known to grumble back in unison, like dogs howling at a police siren. Shallow quakes can also cause tsunamis, which devastated Southeast Asia in December 2004. Created by an uplifting of the ocean floor, these waves travel 500 miles per hour toward shore, but to animals in the deep ocean they're just a passing ripple.

● ● ● ● ● ● ● ●

Q: What's the oldest manmade object in space?

—*STACEY YATES, SUGAR LAND, TEXAS*

A: The Methuselah of space stuff is Vanguard I, a 3-pound aluminum sphere measuring 6 inches across. Launched by the U.S. Navy in 1958, it was the fourth satellite rocketed into space. (The Soviets' Sputnik I and II were first; the U.S. satellite Explorer I was third.) Dave Williams, a planetary scientist at NASA, says Vanguard I wasn't much to look at—Soviet premier Nikita Khrushchev mocked it as the "grapefruit satellite"—but it did have serious scientific aims, such as testing the viability of solar-cell batteries in space. Vanguard I went silent in 1964, but since it orbited much higher than its predecessors—well above the atmospheric drag that slowed the other satellites down and caused them to decay sooner—that little grapefruit won't burn up for at least two hundred years.

METEOROLOGY, ASTRONOMY, AND THE MOON

Q: When will the next ice age occur?
—*NED DURDEN, CHARLOTTE, NORTH CAROLINA*

A: You can relax, Ned. Glaciers aren't expected to swallow up major real estate on the continents for another 80,000 years. Over the last 2.5 million years or so, ice ages have returned, fairly consistently, every 100,000 years. They're caused by subtle changes in the Earth's orbit and its distance from the sun, factors that decrease the amount of sunlight striking the planet, which allows the ice to creep south. But that's not the whole story, says NOAA paleoclimatologist David Anderson. An ice age also requires "feedbacks," which amplify the cooling. One prime example: the albedo effect, whereby ice reflects sunlight, causing more cooling, which makes for bigger glaciers. Other variables play a part, like the amount of carbon-dioxide-consuming plankton on the ocean surface. Since we humans are in the process of increasing CO_2 amounts, you might wonder whether global warming will ever make ice ages a thing of the past. Good question! Anderson says. Chillingly, nobody knows.

Q: I've heard it's sometimes possible to see stars during the middle of the day. True?

—GABRIEL BROWNE, SANTA FE, NEW MEXICO

A: The trick here is knowing exactly where to look. On a very clear day, a skilled stargazer can view the brightest stars with a telescope or even binoculars trained on just the right spot. When it comes to doing it with the naked eye, many seasoned astronomers say it's absurd, but some grant that it's conceivable. U.S. Naval Observatory astronomer Jeff Chester, for one, says he's done it. Chester claims that on a day of "great transparency," at the telescope village on the top of Hawaii's Mauna Kea, he once viewed Arcturus, the fourth-brightest star (not counting our sun). "The sky was a deep, deep blue in the middle of the afternoon," he says, and at his 13,760-foot perch he was above 90 percent of the water vapor in the atmosphere. "It was right where it was supposed to be—I'm sure it was Arcturus." But don't scorch your retinas scanning the skies. "They were very special conditions," Chester says. "I guarantee you're not going to see Arcturus from downtown Washington, D.C."

Q: What would happen if we lost our moon?

—*AMANDA CARLSON, DAKOTA, ILLINOIS*

A: Rest assured, there's no reason to fear that this may happen. But for the sake of argument, if the moon were to go AWOL, life on Earth would become a different ballgame. Neil Comins, an astrophysicist at the University of Maine, says the oceans' tides would immediately become a third as strong, severely threatening life in the intertidal zone. This could also affect fish like the grunion, which spawn according to tidal changes. Sea turtle hatchlings, which use moonlight to find their way to the ocean, would be in trouble. But the most profound effect over the long haul would be the changes in the Earth's obliquity—the angle of its spin axis—which is stabilized by the moon's gravitational pull. Says NASA astrobiologist Kevin Zahnle, over millions of years the planet would wobble chaotically, which could mean ice caps in Miami. As if moonless walks on the beach weren't unromantic enough.

* * * * * * * *

Q: What is the Specter of the Brocken, and what causes it?

—*MIKE BROWN, BELLINGHAM, WASHINGTON*

A: Named for Germany's foggy 3,747-foot Brocken Peak, where climbers have observed it for centuries, this optical effect—also called a mountain specter—usually occurs when you're high above a heavy cloud or fog bank and the sun is directly behind you, conditions rare enough that many mountaineers have never seen one, though airline passengers flying above clouds often witness specters of the planes they're on. If you ever see the Specter, which looks like a giant human figure, what you're witnessing is your shadow projected onto the cloud, usually surrounded by multicolored rings, or "glories," so as to resemble an angelic vision. But you haven't arrived at the pearly gates. As Jeffrey Lew, an atmospheric scientist at UCLA, explains, when sunlight hits the backs of water droplets and bounces back, it skims the surface of the drops; this can cause inter-ference, which appears to us in the form of rings. "In the old days, only climbers saw them, and they got really freaked out," says Lew. "Now all you have to do is look out from your window seat as you nurse a Bloody Mary."

* * * * * * * *

Q: Is it possible to see the North Star and the Southern Cross from the same spot?

—KIRK MASON, RIO RANCHO, NEW MEXICO

A: For those who snoozed through Astronomy 101, the North Star, a.k.a. Polaris, which sits above the north celestial pole, and the Southern Cross, a crucifix-shaped constellation that points to the North Star's counterpart, Sigma Octanis, have been crucial navigational aids through the ages. Yes, you can see them at the same time—you could even build a nice vacation around it. "Try Jamaica from March till June,"

METEOROLOGY, ASTRONOMY, AND THE MOON

says Geoff Chester, an astronomer at the U.S. Naval
Observatory, in Washington, D.C. During those months,
Westerners can see the Southern Cross up to about 22
degrees north—e.g., the upper Caribbean. The North Star is
visible year-round if you're situated more than 5 degrees
north of the equator. South of that, it's usually too close to
the horizon to be seen—a fact that European sailors learned
the hard way when sailing the planet's midsection.

* * * * * * * *

Q: Can any telescope see the U.S. flag on the moon?

—*Bruce Halliday, Shrewsbury, Massachusetts*

A: To spot the flag planted by Neil Armstrong and Buzz
Aldrin—or any of the other five flags Americans left on the
moon between 1969 and 1972—you'd need perfect observ-
ing conditions and a telescope with an aperture as big as
five football fields. But before you call Very Large
Telescopes 'R' Us, be aware that perfect conditions can't
exist on Earth. Even on the clearest night, from the highest
peak, says Boston University astronomer Amanda Bosh, no
scope could possibly see through our planet's gauzy, shift-
ing atmosphere and spy those 3-by-5-foot banners. And
that's assuming they're still there. Don't tell Francis Scott
Key, but given that the moon's weak atmosphere can't block
micro-meteorites and ultraviolet rays, the flags may have
disintegrated long ago.

Q: What's the windiest place in the solar system?

—AMY WADDELL, LOS ANGELES, CALIFORNIA

A: If Winnie the Pooh took in a blustery day on Neptune, he would become Winnie the Projectile—wind speeds there routinely reach 900 miles per hour in the atmosphere. (Neptune being a giant ball of gas, it has no surface on which to measure surface wind speed.) Why is the eighth planet from the sun so blowy? We don't know.

According to Adam Showman, a planetary-science professor at the University of Arizona, scientists can estimate wind speeds on distant orbs by tracking the movement of clouds and dust, but they don't know why one planet is windier than another. While they sort that out, chalk up one more reason to appreciate life on Earth. While the fastest recorded wind here, occurring a few hundred feet above the ground in an Oklahoma tornado, was a hair-raising 318 miles per hour, the average wind speed on the surface is a much more bearable 10 to 20 mph.

METEOROLOGY, ASTRONOMY, AND THE MOON

Chapter 2

NATURE...
You're
Soaking in It
YOUR BODY,
THE BACKCOUNTRY

Q: Is it safe to drink out of plastic bottles?

—*Anonymous*

A: After a widely circulated, government-funded 2003 study linked chromosome damage in the eggs of female mice with bisphenol-A (BPA)—a component in polycarbonate containers like those ubiquitous hard-plastic water bottles, baby bottles, and water-cooler jugs—more scientists entered the fray to argue over the health effects on humans. The debate remains open: A number of independent studies suggest cause for concern, but it will be years before any consensus emerges. According to the National Toxicology Program, both sides in this fierce debate have "credible" points. It would be premature to avoid polycarbonate, but for now, if you have older containers that are scratched or cracked, and thus more likely to leach BPA (as well as harbor bacteria), follow plastic manufacturers' suggestions and get new ones. Finally, it's best to hand-wash your bottles in soap and water.

Q: I've heard that it's possible to survive in the wild by eating snow and drinking your own urine. True?

—MARK STEFANELLI, SEASIDE, OREGON

A: Since snow is nothing more than standard-issue H_2O packaged in crystal form, you can gorge on all the white stuff in your neighborhood, so long as you use common sense (i.e., don't eat snow that's the color of snowblower exhaust). But in an acute survival situation, there are more important guidelines to follow. According to Peter Hackett, the world's foremost high-altitude physician, the first rule is to determine how you feel. Hackett advises against eating snow if you're shivering or if you were previously shivering and now feel lethargic or delirious, all warning signs of hypothermia. Eating snow will only lower your already plummeting core temperature. (Let it fall to 60 degrees Fahrenheit and you're never going to warm up.) As for alternative beverages like, well, your own pee . . . don't even think about it. While urine is 95 percent water, the other 5 percent consists of diuretic urea, creatine, and several other waste products. Each sour slurp restokes your body with the same salts and acids it was trying to expel; your kidneys produce more urine and you grow even thirstier. So do yourself a favor and resist the allure of a tinkle cocktail—even if the producer of *Survivor III* tells you it'll make great TV.

Q: Perhaps you can resolve a dispute between myself (short) and a friend (tall). He claims a tall man can do fewer pull-ups than a short man because the tall man pulls a longer distance to the bar. I say a tall man puts forth the same effort, since taller men have bigger muscles. Who is right?

—*Tim Anderson, St. Coal Valley, Illinois*

A: Assuming a similar level of fitness, diet, and body shape, the taller person has a disadvantage when it comes to pull-ups. But don't let your pal gloat—the height handicap has nothing to do with distance from chin to bar, but rather with a frustrating fact of physiology: When you grow, you add weight in all directions—getting thicker and taller—but your muscle gets stronger only as it grows thicker. "Muscle force has been found to correspond to the two-dimensional cross-section of a muscle, measured across the muscle fibers," explains University of California–Davis exercise biology professor Keith Williams. "Weight is proportionate to body volume, measured in three dimensions."

Simply put, taller people have bigger muscles, but they have less muscle to lift more weight. To illustrate gravity's triumph over human development, look no further than the women's division of the American Sport Climbing Federation Nationals. Last June, the muscle-bound, 5-foot, 4-inch champ Tiffany Campbell nearly lost to 4-foot, 9-inch Tori Allen—a 65-pound 12-year-old. *(Contributed by Stephanie Pearson)*

＊　　＊　　＊　　＊　　＊　　＊　　＊　　＊

Q: Is a $50 shirt with a 50+ SPF rating more protective than my old Iron Maiden T-shirt?

—JIM COX, BIRMINGHAM, ALABAMA

A: All the clothing in your wardrobe (save for the mesh muscle shirt) provides some protection from the sun's ultraviolet rays. Its effectiveness is indicated by its UPF, or ultraviolet protection factor. Similar to a sunscreen's SPF, UPF gauges how much UV radiation can pass through a garment. Created in 1996 by the Australian Radiation Protection and Nuclear Safety Agency (Australia being the skin-cancer capital of the world), the UPF standard is used by apparel makers all over the world. Seattle-based Ex Officio's Sunblock shirts are UPF 30, meaning they let through one-thirtieth of all UV rays—considered adequately protective. (A new white T-shirt has a UPF of only 5.) Royal Robbins makes 40+ shirts, and the GoSo polo shirt, made Down Under by the Sun Protection Shop, scores the highest rating, 50+. Some clothes are sewn with airier weaves, so you won't sweat to death, and treated with UV-absorbing chemicals like Tinofast. Meanwhile, Rit Sun Guard, which you can throw in the wash cycle, renders your clothes more UV-absorbing—it's like lathering them up with SPF 30 lotion, without the greasy feeling. If you're loyal to the basic cotton tee, stick with black: Dark colors feel hotter, but they absorb more of those killer UV rays.

.   .   .   .

Q: What fabric will keep you cooler in hot weather: cotton, which retains sweat, or a high-tech synthetic that wicks it away?

—ANONYMOUS

A: Admirers of each material have their own strong opinions, but the textile scientists we talked to said cotton and high-tech fabrics perform about the same during exercise in warm conditions. In a 2001 study from Indiana University's Human Performance Laboratory, eight "well-trained males" wearing cotton and evaporative synthetics were monitored as they walked and ran in moderately dry 85-degree air. No difference was found in the subjects' core temperatures. So it really comes down to comfort. The whole idea behind those technical garments is to keep you dry, which is the right strategy for Central Park but not the Grand Canyon. On a nice breezy day in the Canyon, being clammy could feel pretty good, so cotton would be a wise move. Just be sure to change by nightfall, when the mercury plunges.

Q: How should I choose my bottled water?

—ADAM SUSSMAN, NEW YORK, NEW YORK

A: Daunting, isn't it? All those varieties, all those claims to being the purest—how is a thirsty athlete to decide? Saving any talk of "enhanced" fitness waters for another day, let's look at the health benefits of the two basic kinds: water with stuff, and water without. First there's mineral water, which contains 250 parts per million of dissolved solids like calcium, magnesium, and zinc that have been acquired from underground deposits. (Spring waters, depending on where the spring flows, may have enough mineral content to go in this category, or may be much, much purer.) Eileen Vincent, a nutritionist at Northwestern University, in Evanston, Illinois, confirms that these minerals are a boon to your system but says that since any brand has only a fraction of the stuff you need, it'll never be a substitute for your leafy greens and whole grains. Then there's what we'll call pure water, which has few or no minerals. Mother Nature's purest comes from glaciers and from springs in Norway and Fiji, but most pure bottled water gets that way through filtering processes like reverse osmosis. Whether it comes from Fiji or a filter, says Vincent, it's neither better nor worse than mineral water from a nutrition standpoint. In other words, they're all good for you, so you're free to base your decision on flavor.

Q: Is it true that the Inuit have 20 different words for snow?

—C. KNUTSEN, NEW YORK, NEW YORK

A: At least 20, depending on your dictionary. According to *The Kobuk Iñupiaq Dictionary*, used in schools throughout northwestern Alaska, there are 23 words in the Inuit language, Iñupiaq, to describe winter's powdery precip.

Only three—*qannik, aniu,* and *apun*—specifically translate as "snow on the ground." The other 20 detail myriad other snowy incarnations, among them *auksalak* ("melting snow") and *pukak* ("sugar snow thawed to make drinking water"). How can so few syllables say so much? Unlike English, Iñupiaq is a polysynthetic language—dozens of affixes can add nuance to the meaning of a simple noun like snow. According to *West Greenlandic,* an Inuit dictionary that has a whopping 49 words for both snow and ice, *qanipalaat* means "feathery clumps of falling snow," and then there's *qiqsruqqaq* ("glaze on snow in thaw time"), and the deadly *sisuuk* ("wet snow that can slide and cause an avalanche"). "Our lives," explains Lorena Williams Kapniaq, an Iñupiaq instructor at the University of Alaska–Fairbanks, "are centered around snow."

Q: When I fly my paraglider I sometimes see a bright light where my shadow should be. Am I glowing?

—ERIC REED, SAN FRANCISCO, CALIFORNIA

A: Uh, no, but you are having a lesson in the bizarre, little-known science of atmospheric optics. This enlightening phenomenon is called a dry heiligenschein, or "holy light," and you don't have to leave the ground to observe one. On a sunny day, stand on some grass and look at the shadow of your head. Just outside the shadow you'll notice a halo; it's bright there because you're looking directly along the lines of the sun's rays and can't see the shadows cast by the leaves of grass. Now look several inches outside the halo. There, the rays are striking the grass at an angle with respect to your line of sight, so you can see the grass cast little shadows off to the side; the effect is darker-looking grass. Put the two phenomena together—the halo and the shadow ring—and the contrast causes the halo to appear even brighter. As a paraglider, you'll witness the same effect when the sun is high and you're soaring over a grassland, thick forest, wheat field, or other similarly shaggy surface—but as you gain altitude, your shadow will shrink until it disappears, the bright spot will take its place, and a heavenly specter will follow you below.

Q Why doesn't the hair on your eyelids need trimming?

—*Scott Myers, New York, New York*

A: "The answer," says Sarah Millar, a professor of dermatology at the University of Pennsylvania, "is right in front of your eyes: Eyelashes don't have to be trimmed because they don't grow very long." They're programmed, Millar explains, to reach only a certain length—about ¼ inch—and then stop. Any longer and they'd be more a hindrance (obscuring your vision) than a benefit (protecting against dust and light). Like all human hair, eyelashes go through a three-part growth cycle. In the first phase, called anagen, they grow from tiny follicles in the skin; next, they stop growing and the follicles go dormant; finally, the hair clings to the follicles until being shed. All hair grows at the same rate, so length depends on how much time is spent in the growing stage: a few months for eyelashes and body hair, several years for scalp hair. Or perhaps forever, if you're Willie Nelson.

Q: Are there mammals besides humans that do not naturally know how to swim?

—KAREN STEWART, MERIDIAN, IDAHO

A: Well, scientists would argue that humans do innately know how to swim. Most infants are capable of flailing their arms and legs enough to keep their heads above water for at least a short time. "Babies don't swim very well because their motor skills are not fully developed," admits Frank Fish (pure coincidence), an expert on the energetics of swimming at Pennsylvania's West Chester University. "But all humans have a layer of fat, smooth skin, and the ability to breath-hold"—attributes that make us quite aquatically suited. Similarly, most four-legged mammals can turn their walking strides into an ungainly dog paddle if necessary. The notable exceptions are giraffes and apes. The reason for the giraffe's inability to swim is painfully self-evident: Like a keel without a hull, the long-necked creature simply cannot stay upright in water.

Orangutans, gorillas, and their ape relatives, meanwhile, will ineffectually thrash around in deep water or simply gurgle and sink. (After more than half a dozen accidental ape drownings in the past decade, modern zoos have caught on and surrounded their moats with electric fences.) Of course, there is little scientific data on this apparent evolutionary oversight. "Throwing a chimpanzee in the water and watching it drown is not the sort of experiment we like to do," says Fish. *(Contributed by Stephanie Pearson)*

* * * * * * * *

Q: **Is there really such a thing as a runner's high? I've been a long-distance runner for years, and I've never experienced it.**

—*ERIC KESZLER, CORDOVA, TENNESSEE*

A: The term "runner's high" has been around since the jogging craze took off in the mid-1970s and is used to describe anything from a mildly elevated mood to a narcotic-like euphoria that might come over you during or after any hard workout. While the sheer number of people who claim to have experienced this buzz points to something more than a placebo effect, science has yet to verify or explain it. Conventional wisdom attributes the high to the brain's release of morphine-like chemicals called endorphins. But Virginia Grant, a psychology professor at Memorial University of Newfoundland, thinks a more complex cocktail of brain chemicals is at work. Her studies found that rats seem to experience pleasure when running on a wheel—which indicates a probable endorphin rush—and she points to earlier tests showing that, if given the chance, a rat will run itself to death, as if literally addicted. This suggested to Grant that dopamine, a major chemical behind addictive behavior, may be present as well. If this is true for humans, then it may be that those folks with more addictive personalities are likely to experience a runner's high, while others might only feel somewhat better. Check back in a few years.

*   *   *   *   *   *   *   *

Q: Why do we say "Geronimo" when we jump?

—MARIAN MILLER, SANTA FE, NEW MEXICO

A: We humans like to yell battle cries before entering the fray—be it bona fide war or a cannonball off the high dive—as a way of raising our confidence and unifying the ranks. This particular utterance dates back to 1940 and a U.S. Army paratrooper named Aubrey Eberhardt. On the eve of the Army's first mass parachute jump, at Fort Benning, Georgia, he and his platoon watched a B-grade western called Geronimo, about the 19th-century Chiricahua Apache chief. Private Eberhardt was inspired by the fierce warrior and told his buddies he was going to shout "Geronimo!" when he jumped the next day to get out the jitters. He did just that, followed by a war whoop. The others did the same, and soon the cry was being heard all over the skies above Normandy—and at swimming holes all across America.

Q: Why do parts of my body sometimes feel cold to the touch when I don't actually feel cold in those places?

—Julie Colhoun, San Francisco, California

A: The feeling of being cold—a sensation brought on when your core temperature is threatened but at 98.6 degrees is still quite warm—and finding your skin cold to the touch are two very different things, caused by two separate physiological processes. In fact, cold skin (usually found in fatty areas like the stomach, thighs, cheeks, and buttocks) helps you feel warmer on the inside. Here's how: The body protects its vital organs from the cold by retaining as much heat as possible within its core. In environments below 65 degrees Fahrenheit, your circulatory system limits the amount of 98.6-degree blood flowing to your outer layers through a process called vasoconstriction: Smooth muscles in the tiny arteries of the skin contract, and this narrowing decreases blood flow, curtailing heat loss, while making your outermost layer feel cold to the touch. But because vasoconstriction only slows the loss of heat from your core, it can't keep you toasty on its own if you stay out too long or if the temperature drops even 5 degrees more. If cool turns to cold, your core temperature becomes threatened and your insides start to feel like your outsides—chilly. Your adrenal glands kick in, your metabolism quickens, and the extra energy burned warms your core.

(Contributed by Stephanie Pearson)

Q: How do you officially name a mountain? Can I name a peak near my house "Bob"?

—*Oliver Slesar, Cambridge, Massachusetts*

A: Call the peak (or creek or prairie) anything you'd like, but if you want to see the name on a government-issue map, be prepared to scale the Everest-like flanks of the federal bureaucracy. "You know, a name is a lasting thing," says Roger L. Payne, executive secretary of the U.S. Board on Geographic Names, "so the process is lengthy by design." First, visit the board's Web site at geonames.usgs .gov, and fill out—surprise—a long, involved form. Provide a description of the hill, its longitude and latitude, your reason for wanting to name it, the meaning of the name, evidence that the peak isn't already named, and the name you propose. (Bear in mind, they won't name a natural feature after a living person: "You never know what a person might do in the future. He or she might disgrace him- or herself," adds Payne.) The Board, after pestering you with questions, will render its decision three to six months later, accepting approximately 90 percent of the proposals. The secret of success? Make sure locals like the name. Says Payne, "We're not going to anger a whole county just so we can name something 'Bob.'" Of course, even then there's no guarantee your name will be popular. Many people still call Alaska's highest peak Denali, despite its official name, Mount McKinley.

Q: How much horsepower can a human generate?

—*DIMITY MCDOWELL, SANTA FE, NEW MEXICO*

A: British engineer James Watt coined the term *horsepower* in 1809 for the amount of power a pony puts out when hauling a bucket of coal from the ground. It remains the official imperial unit of power, and it's defined as the work required to raise 550 pounds a distance of 1 foot in 1 second. Determining how much horsepower a human can generate while skiing or hiking or cycling is complex—considerably more complex than, say, measuring the horsepower of a car engine by hooking it up to a dynamometer. But there are devices, like the computer on a rowing machine, that keep track of this sort of thing. According to one biomechanist's findings, elite sprinters typically generate just over one horsepower when accelerating off the blocks, and Russian Andrei Chemerkin, possibly the world's strongest man, generated 5.84 horsepower when clean-and-jerking 556.5 pounds in 1999. Scientists can also determine the amount of horsepower a human generates by working backwards, converting horsepower into more easily measured units such as BTUs or even dietary calories. They've found the heart is neither lean nor mean; it's a 0.008-horsepower machine. And the human brain, site of millions of electrochemical explosions per second, is only slightly more potent, at 0.02 horsepower—about the same as a low-wattage light bulb.

Q: When I dream that I'm exercising, does my body respond physiologically?

—MIKE BUCKLEY, STATE COLLEGE, PENNSYLVANIA

A: In a word, nope. Most of your muscles are in a quasi-paralyzed state during REM (rapid eye movement) sleep, when vivid dreaming takes place. According to Jerome Siegel, a professor of psychiatry and behavioral sciences at UCLA's Center for Sleep Research, the human brain, probably as a result of evolution, turns off the motor neurons so we won't injure ourselves or our sleeping partners—and so predators won't be drawn by our movements. While some people suffer from REM behavior disorder, in which the muscles don't shut off properly and the subject moves around or sleepwalks, we have yet to hear of anyone sleep-running a 10K. Vital signs such as heart rate may be affected by dream content, so visions of Sugar Ray Robinson sparring with you probably have a different effect than visions of strolling down a beach; still, without any muscle contraction, the fitness factor would be nil. This leaves the rather subjective idea that an exercise dream can make you feel better. To date, no studies have addressed endorphin rushes in sleeping people. Our take: If you dream you've just claimed the yellow jersey from Lance, more power to you, but the chances that it's made you fitter are about as good as if you'd sat through *Breaking Away* for the ninth time.

Q: Can you fall asleep while walking?

—KRISTA HURCOMB, MINNEAPOLIS, MINNESOTA

A: "You can sleep while you're walking," says Jerry Siegel, a psychologist at UCLA's Sleep Research Center, "but of course, you can't get REM or restful sleep." In other words: Yes, worry about walking off a cliff at the end of a long hike; no, you can't trek the whole Appalachian Trail in dreamland. EEGs show that during a groggy state called microsleep, activity in the cortex momentarily slows down and then seconds later speeds up to normal. Your brain goes offline, online, and then offline again. Ultimately, however, after prolonged periods of semiwakefulness, your fatigued body and brain will agree on the need for deep sleep—crucial for restoring muscles, organizing memories, and regulating moods—and you'll simply conk out. People can delay microsleep and the impulse to rest by exerting themselves (think of adventure racers), but, as Michael Perlis, director of the University of Rochester's Sleep Research Laboratory, points out, if you were strong enough to run on adrenaline for weeks, you'd be terminally fit: "Total sleep deprivation is probably fatal." *(Contributed by Stephanie Pearson)*

Q: Why does my iPod stop working when I climb fourteeners?

—ANONYMOUS

A: Two things can go wrong. Like all devices powered by a lithium-ion battery, an iPod will shut down when the temperature is cold enough to neutralize the ion-transferring chemical reaction in the battery. Warmth will revive it. With a hard-disk-based music player like the iPod, thin air is a bigger threat. These units store data on a hard drive that spins at 4,200 rpm while a head floats nanometers above it, reading data. As air pressure drops, the air cushion has fewer molecules to sustain it; take it high enough and you risk a "head crash," in which head and disk collide, damaging your song library. Apple advises a ceiling of 10,000 feet for the 'Pod, but climbers on Everest have successfully busted out the jams as high as 21,000 feet. Push the envelope if you dare, but Chet Baker might not be there for you at the top.

Q: Why is lichen put into natural deodorant?

—SARAH BOVEY, SUNDERLAND, VERMONT

A: Press your nose against a lichen-covered rock and you might detect a pleasant herbal smell. But the reason the crusty plant is used in deodorant has more to do with science and folklore than with its subtle perfume. First, the science: Every lichen is actually two organisms—a fungus and an alga—living in symbiosis and exchanging food, water, and minerals with each other. Among the dozens of chemicals that lichens produce (from naturally occurring sugars) are acids designed to kill invading microbes that might be harmful to the relationship—hence the theory, among some scientists, that these same acids are capable of killing the odor-causing bacteria that flourish around your sweat glands during a long trail run. It's not a new notion: For 2,000-plus years, lichens have been thought to wield curative powers. The lichen known as old man's beard, which drapes the branches of oak and pine trees from North America to China, was used to treat whooping cough, cataracts, dropsy, and epilepsy, in addition to being considered an astringent, a tonic, a diuretic, a remedy for baldness, and a salve that could heal battle wounds. Today, you'll find this once ubiquitous cure-all in homeopathic prescriptions for headaches—and as a key ingredient in Tom's of Maine deodorant.

Q: I was riding my bike the other morning and accidentally inhaled a bug. Is there a big pile of assorted bug parts in my lungs?

—JEFF EISKEN, FORT SMITH, ARKANSAS

A: If indeed you are worried, don't be. Your lungs, while prone to harboring an insect or two, have a built-in bug-removal process. Assuming the critter isn't a 2.5-ounce giant weta from New Zealand (considered by many to be the world's largest insect), rest assured that the hairlike structures in your airway, called cilia, will work in sequence to brush microscopic bug bits up the trachea so you can cough them out. It's unlikely that the little corpse will make it all the way down your windpipe, but if it does, your lungs will activate an emergency backup plan. "Your body recognizes the bug as foreign," explains Armando Huaringa, a pulmonologist and member of the American Association for Bronchology. "Your lungs encapsulate the bug with mucus, and over time the proteins get broken down by chemical processes." This pulmonary entombment leaves a small tumor on the lung, called a granuloma—but fear not, it's benign, more granola than melanoma. On the other hand, aspirant pneumonia is a remote possibility if the bug carried bacteria. Ideally, though, the pharynx—a trapdoor at the back of the mouth—has already diverted the errant bit of vermin down your esophagus and into your belly, away from your windpipe. "Your stomach is better equipped than your lungs for this kind of work," says Huaringa.

Q: Do people sweat when they swim?

—*JAMI KEI MARKLE, GRAND MARAIS, MINNESOTA*

A: That's affirmative, says Louise Burke, a dietitian at the Australian Institute of Sport, in Canberra. Burke recently published a study in which 64 swimmers and water-polo players were weighed before and after their workouts, and found that they lost an average of 14 ounces of sweat per hour—much less than the 50 ounces leaked by a typical marathoner, but plenty of drippage all the same. Of course, since evaporation doesn't occur underwater, perspiring—which is the body's way of releasing excess heat generated by exertion—doesn't do much good for swimmers. But they shouldn't sweat it. A body moving in water loses heat at a rate 60 to 80 times faster than in air, so direct heat transfer, mostly through convection, cools swimmers down as they churn.

Q: Is human hair a good insulator?

—*NATHAN JOHNSON, LOS ANGELES, CALIFORNIA*

A: A material's ability to keep you warm is a function of how much air it can trap. The trapped air, not the fiber itself, does the insulating. According to Yash Kamath, a materials scientist at TRI/Princeton, a New Jersey–based textile-research institute, the more crimped a fiber is, the more open structure it has for holding air. Wool, for example, is far more twisty than human hair—even a Rastafarian's—so although both fibers are made of the protein keratin, a wool hat will keep heat in far better than any head of hair. But before you start rethinking your hat inventory, be advised that the oft-cited claim that you lose most of your heat through your head is a myth. In fact, only 10 percent of your heat leaks out via the noggin, says Daniel Sessler, an anesthesiologist at the University of Louisville School of Medicine. It was a faulty 1950s study, coupled with the head's sensitivity to cold, that gave rise to the belief. A hat is a smart choice, but it's no more crucial than any other skin-covering item.

* * * * * * * *

Q: What is the most nutrient-rich food in the world?

—ANONYMOUS

A: Nature's great, but it doesn't provide one single food that gives you everything. So depending on which nutrients you consider most crucial, the answer may be eggs, soybeans, avocadoes, or—if it suits your age group—breast milk. But if you want to nail down the two main categories—macronutrients (protein, carbs, and fats) and micronutrients (vitamins and minerals)—try using a little teamwork. According to University of California–Davis nutritionist Britt Burton-Freeman, nuts are packed with protein and healthy fats, as well as certain vitamins and minerals (almonds are great for vitamin E, walnuts for potassium). To get your carbs and a potent cocktail of micronutrients, add any colorful dried fruit, such as vitamin-C-rich dried strawberries. There are plenty of conveniently packaged performance and nutrition bars containing all these beneficial things, but whatever the source, it's ultimately Mother Nature's good work.

* * * * * * * *

Q: Do any cannibalistic societies exist today?
—*CRAIG COLLINS, SANTA ROSA, CALIFORNIA*

A: The two tribes known to have practiced cannibalism most recently are the Fore of Papua New Guinea and the Wari of western Brazil, both of which had given up eating people by the 1960s, at the urging of colonizers. "The Wari ate their enemies after warfare as a way of expressing anger and disdain for them," says Vanderbilt University anthropology professor Beth Conklin, who lived with the Wari in the 1980s and

Ogo, wipe your face, you have a piece of your cousin stuck to it!

interviewed many onetime cannibals. "They also consumed members of their own group who died naturally, out of respect." Anthropologists aren't aware of any cannibalism occurring today, but a lot depends on your definition of the term. The Yanomami of the Amazon, for example, still practice osteophagy, the consuming of the ground bones of one's relatives after cremation as a symbol of affection, or as a way of invoking the ancestor's spirit before going into battle to avenge his death. "When you study its various uses, you realize that cannibalism isn't as disgusting as you originally thought," says Conklin. Stop right there, professor. You're beginning to scare us.

* * * * * * * *

Is it true that drinking hot tea or other beverages in hot weather cools you?

—BONNIE SIMON, BERKELEY, CALIFORNIA

A: The logic behind this old wives' tale is convincing: Hot tea, for example, raises one's body temperature, causing the person to sweat more, especially in summer—with evaporation leading to a feeling of coolness. A similar myth holds that the hot-tea-warmed body signals the brain to dilate blood vessels in the skin, which radiates heat and makes the person feel cool. But according to Lawrence Armstrong, professor of exercise and environmental physiology at the University of Connecticut, neither explanation holds water. The laws of thermodynamics dictate that the amount of

body heat lost by sweating or radiation will usually equal—
never exceed—the amount of heat gained by drinking the
hot beverage. The blood-vessel hypothesis is equally
flawed, because when blood vessels in the skin release extra
heat, heat-sensitive nerves in the skin detect that extra heat
and a person will feel flush and hotter. So it's a draw.
(Eating ice cream on a cold day is similarly ineffective.)
"I've tested this theory on dozens of people, and I've never
seen anyone who actually felt more comfortable drinking
hot tea in warm weather," says Armstrong. "You may be
cooler psychologically, but not physiologically."

. . . .

Q: Why can't my eyes focus properly underwater?

—JAMIE SMITH, DENVER, COLORADO

A: When light moves from one medium to another, as it
does when it travels from an object, through the air, and
into your fluid eyeball, the change in resistance makes it
bend. A good thing, considering the human eye has evolved
to accommodate precisely these circumstances: The fluid
behind the cornea refracts light onto the lens; the lens
refracts it again and focuses it clearly onto the retina.
Underwater, however, is another story. Say you're in a river,
washing downstream toward a boulder. Light reflected off
the rock travels through the water, but now, because there's
no change in resistance, it doesn't bend when it hits the eye.

Instead, the lens refracts the light as it does above water—only not enough to correct the off-target ray and snap it into focus. The result is temporary farsighted-ness: The boulder appears as a fuzzy blob. "Our eyes," says National Eye Institute ophthalmologist Richard Hertle, "were only meant to be bathed in tears."

* * * * * * * * *

Q: Looking at a friend's heel blisters made me wonder: Why do people get squeamish?

—*LAVERNE D'ARCY, WINTERVILLE, NORTH CAROLINA*

A: According to Laura Campbell, a therapist at Boston University's Center for Anxiety and Related Disorders, that queasy feeling is actually a triumph of evolution. It tells you, in no uncertain terms, that ripping into flesh isn't healthy. When you witness something gory or smell rotting tissue, your brain fires the neural impulses that give you those heebie-jeebies. You feel both anxious and afraid of contamination—an emotional state psychologists define as disgust. Next, your sympathetic and parasympathetic nerv-ous systems kick in—releasing adrenaline and glucose, raising your heart rate, and pumping larger-than-normal blood flows to the major muscle groups. This mild fight-or-flight response might seem like overkill in the case of a blister or small cut, acknowledges Campbell, but she says it's useful conditioning nonetheless: "Once it's over, you never want to make the same mistake."

* * * * * * * *

Why do some people refer to fishing as "angling"?

—PETER TROLLER, BOULDER, COLORADO

A: Sport fishing dates back 4,000 years to ancient Egypt, but "angling," the word for catching freshwater or saltwater fish with a rod, line, and hook, is derived from the Old English noun *angul*, which means "hook." According to Gary Tanner, executive director for the American Museum of Fly Fishing, in Manchester, Vermont, a later cognate of "angle" appeared in written form in *Parzival*, an early-13th-century chivalric romance by the German author Wolfram von Eschenbach. In it Shionatulander, a young kinsman of King Arthur, catches trout and grayling with a feather-dressed "verderangel," an ancestor of today's Woolly Bugger.

Q: What is the highest unclimbed mountain in the world?

—PHILIP RUSH, ARLINGTON, VIRGINIA

A: If by "mountain" you mean individual massif (as opposed to an outcropping that's part of another mountain), 24,829-foot Gangkar Puensum, on the border between Bhutan and Tibet, currently holds the coveted title. This is according to Joss Lynam, of the International Mountaineering and Climbing Federation, which represents some 88 climbing organizations worldwide and keeps tabs on first ascents (or the lack thereof) of the Earth's loftiest summits. In 1986, two teams—one British, one Austrian—attempted the summit via the South Ridge, but neither was able to top out. So why hasn't the bastard been knocked off since? Two words: religion and politics. For more than 10 years, Bhutan's authoritarian Buddhist government has imposed a country-wide ban on mountaineering, claiming that its peaks are sacred. China, meanwhile, has been less than forthcoming with permits to climb from the Tibetan side. In 1998, a Japanese team *was* granted permission to ascend the peak, but in a textbook example of cryptic Chinese diplomacy, the government "postponed" the permit, citing sensitive border issues. Instead, the climbers got clearance for a successful 1999 bid on 24,711-foot Liankang Kangri, where they were left an agonizing few kilometers away—and just 118 feet below—the highest peak on the same massif, Gangkar Puensum.

Q: What causes you to see stars after a hard blow to the head?

—KENDRA HARPSTER, NEW YORK, NEW YORK

A: Though they usually don't see anything as distinct as the constellation that orbits Wile E. Coyote's head after he's been nailed in the noggin by the obligatory falling anvil, many people see scores of revolving lights, technically called phosphenes, in front of their eyes following a forceful blow to the brain-pan. Problem is, scientists still aren't certain what causes the halluci-nations. James Kelly, a neurolo-gist at the Chicago Neurological Institute, says they've narrowed down the source, suspecting that phosphenes occur when there is "biomechanical irritation" (i.e., a hard whack) to the visual cortex—the area in the occipital lobe, in the rear of the brain, that controls your sight. When it's jarred, scientists posit that temporary physiological and electrical changes there produce the ephemeral celestial visions—sort of the reverse effect of what happens when you slap the television to get better reception.

Q: Are adventure racers who go for days without sleep doing any serious harm to themselves?

—DEBORAH SIMON, SANTA FE, NEW MEXICO

A: Research hasn't revealed any permanent effects on the body resulting from sleep loss, but don't take that as an endorsement for skipping z's. Dr. Claudio Stampi, who's done sleep studies on solo around-the-world sailors at the Chronobiology Research Institute, in Boston, says lack of slumber may not damage any organs, but it will render you a walking (or running) disaster. Studies show that sleepy people make careless decisions, perform routine tasks poorly, and are more accident-prone than the well-rested—all in all, a bad recipe for athletes taking on high-adrenaline sports. Stampi recommends getting no less than four and a half hours of sleep a day, and advises round-the-clock adventure racers to grab their snooze time in "polyphasic" doses (as opposed to the monophasic slumber we typically enjoy)—say, roughly 20 minutes at a time, every hour or two. Since it takes longer to become fully awake after a deep sleep, he explains, "polyphasic sleep will leave you feeling immediately more rested." Of course, anyone who thinks this method will allow him to take on that third or fourth job should think twice. Prolonged sleep deprivation, when coupled with high stress, is one of the most effective forms of torture.

Q: If our body temperature is 98.6 degrees, why does it feel so hot when it's 98 degrees out?

—*SUE WALTON, RIVER FALLS, WISCONSIN*

A: According to University of Kansas exercise physiologist John Thyfault, the temperature of your skin is always a few degrees colder than your internal body temperature. Therefore, air at 98.6 degrees Fahrenheit is hotter than your skin. But more important, says Thyfault, a former college tight end who often practiced with his teammates on artificial turf sunbaked up to 120 degrees, is the role of your nervous system. Scientists believe your brain, nerve networks, and thousands of hot and cold receptors in the skin that gauge the ambient temperature are all prewired to make you feel hot well before the air temperature exceeds that of your skin. Why? Since your body continuously produces excess heat through basic metabolic functions, it's the nervous system's way of making sure you take appropriate action—both voluntary and involuntary—to cool off before you experience heatstroke. In addition to sweating, this means drinking water, throwing in the towel for the day, and—for football squads wanting their quarterback to pass, not pass out—getting off the scorching turf.

Q: Why are there such individualized names for groups of animals: gaggles of geese, packs of wolves, herds of sheep, etc.?

—ANDY AND ALISA MALLINGER, PORTLAND, OREGON

A: If you've ever taken up a sport and suddenly found your vocabulary becoming much larger (*abseil, 'biner, belay* . . .), then you may understand how these terms came into being. In the Middle Ages, the collective nouns given to animals were likewise part of the lingo of a sport: hunting. They were dubbed "terms of venery" (from the Old French word *vener,* meaning "to hunt"), and their use was tied to the Forest Laws, a set of guidelines written to protect the animals on the king's hunting lands. The first major reference to these words in literature appears in Thomas Malory's 1485 King Arthur classic *Le Morte d'Arthur,* in which Sir Tristram is said to know "all the good terms of venery and hunting . . . and of him we had all the terms of hawking, and which were beasts of chase and beasts of venery." In other words, Tristram knew a clowder from a murder, and therefore he was somebody. Some of the names are more generic (a gang of elk), others are anthropomorphic (a parliament of owls), and some are downright poetic (an exaltation of larks). While they make for funny dinner conversation now, in days of yore these words were taken very seriously. "Hunting animals and birds was a noble sport," says Allan Metcalf, an English professor at MacMurray College, in Jacksonville, Illinois, "and it was noble to know all of the various terms of the hunt."

Q: Is human skin waterproof and breathable?

—*Mike Callaghan, Toronto, Ontario*

A: In other words, is your skin like a naturally occurring Gore-Tex jacket? The answer, according to Dr. Robert Polisky, a dermatologist in Elk Grove Village, Illinois, is both yes and no. Skin, which protects the body against injury, microorganisms, and chemical agents, is water-resistant but not waterproof. The protective layer is called the stratum corneum, a thin membrane of mostly dead cells that's rich in a protein called keratin and also coated with sebum, an oil secreted through hair follicles. Together they create a water-resistant barrier that protects the dermis, where the capillaries and sweat glands lie. (If you want to verify that your skin isn't waterproof, take a long bath—the prunelike effect on your hands and feet is a result of the keratin becoming waterlogged.) So does your skin breathe?

Not in a strict sense: Your pores don't inhale or exhale. But they do allow harmful metabolic wastes like salt and urea to escape the body when it heats up. Thus, the skin, which weighs an average of 6.5 pounds, may be heavier than a high-performance jacket, but it has at least one distinct advantage: You never need to take it to the dry cleaner.

*   *   *   *   *   *   *   *

Q: Are humans born with all of their bones?

—JUSTIN BERRY, BEMIDJI, MINNESOTA

A: Sort of. While we come into the world with a complete skeletal system, about 50 percent of it starts out as cartilage, which is much softer and more flexible than bone—a definite plus when it comes to squeezing through the birth canal, says Hans-Georg Simon, a developmental biologist at Northwestern University's Feinberg School of Medicine, in Chicago. Cartilage is also quite handy because it allows the bones to harden gradually—or "ossify," in white-coat lingo—as a baby bounces on into childhood. In some places, such as the hands and the skull—picture the soft spot on a baby's head—several infant bones fuse together and form new, larger bones. So, over time, we actually go from having about 300 bones (some of them cartilaginous) down to 206. By the end of puberty, when most of your cartilage has hardened, bones stop growing longer and your skeleton is a finished work of art.

Q: What is the advantage of height in humans? Or is there an advantage to a lack of height?

—MARY JO BURKE, NEW YORK, NEW YORK

A: It's tough to say, especially since most of us don't live according to the severe and unwavering demands of the wild; i.e., we don't need long legs to outstride ill-tempered rhinos or long arms to reach the upper branches of trees. And even among those who live in harsh environments, shortness can be a boon. Inuit, for example, are blessed with a compact build that helps them retain body heat in the frigid North. Height is always an advantage in one domain, however: social prestige. "Any animal that lives in a social group dominates if it is bigger than the others," says Barry

Bogin, an anthropologist from the University of Michigan–Dearborn and author of *The Growth of Humanity*, a study of both the physical and demographic growth of human populations. "Larger animals dominate in competition for food, mating partners, and nesting space. With humans, tall salespeople tend to get hired in lieu of shorter colleagues, and they receive higher starting salaries." Of course, this is true only to a certain point (the beanpole jokes definitely fly after 7 feet), though you'd be hard-pressed to say exactly why, without dissecting our deepest animal brains. (*Contributed by Stephanie Pearson*)

Q: **I recently climbed 14,162-foot Mount Shasta, and had a hard time eating. What happens to appetite up high?**

—JOHN ADAMS II, FREMONT, CALIFORNIA

A: It disappears into (ahem) thin air. Researchers are largely stumped as to why, but they know that hypoxia, or oxygen deprivation, can cause drastic bodily changes. On the appetite front, scientists are focusing on three hormones that regulate hunger—galanin, neuropeptide Y, and leptin. Leptin seems to be especially crucial: As you climb above 9,000 feet, your fat cells start overproducing it, which tells the hypothalamus that you're full. Careful acclimatization may ameliorate the problem, but that takes time. And since there are no drugs—save cannabis—proven to stimulate appetite, you've simply got to force those nibbles. Even if it seems impossible, stresses altitude specialist Dr. Peter Hackett, you need to choke down something, in small portions, the more calories the better: energy gels, sweets, pastas dripping with chutney. If you don't, you'll start burning muscle, and that can be catastrophic.

Q: What percentage of the U.S. is paved?

—*Jessica LeClair, Windsor Locks, Connecticut*

A: If you count only roads, says Richard Forman, a Harvard professor of landscape ecology, the number is 0.6 percent, an area roughly half the size of Virginia. If you throw in parking lots, sidewalks, building foundations, and all other "impervious surfaces," the number doubles to about 1.29 percent. That figure may be lower than you expected, but the local effects of too much hardtop can be huge, particularly on the weather. A 1999 NASA study of Atlanta showed that the city's overpaved center has created a "heat island" where daily summertime temperatures can average 8 degrees higher than usual and thunderstorms can occur in the morning—an event almost unheard of before 10-lane highways came along.

Q: Is it still possible to homestead anywhere?

—*LANCE PETERSEN, LOGAN, UTAH*

A: Not in this country. In 1976, Congress repealed the Homestead Act of 1862, which granted 160 acres to anyone who would inhabit and farm it for five years. That said, there are opportunities. Marquette, Kansas, a town looking to rebuild its numbers of young people, is giving away ⅔-acre plots to anybody who moves there and builds a home. Some countries, like India, offer varying amounts of free land to companies or individuals that invest large amounts in local industry—but you probably don't have that kind of scratch. Your most affordable option? The African nation of Zambia. Seeking to ease a decades-long food shortage, that country's government recently started leasing vast swaths of unfarmed land to foreigners for as little as 50 cents an acre (sod house not included).

Q: I've heard coconut juice can be used as a blood substitute—true?

—*Paul Povey, Gig Harbor, Washington*

A: Gilligan, it's a good thing you came to the Professor before trying this. The thin, semisweet "water" inside a coconut (not called milk, which is processed from the coconut meat) can't carry oxygen, so it can't stand in for blood. But it contains important nutrients like glucose, potassium, and calcium, so it can, like saline, be introduced into the blood-stream to rehydrate patients who are unable to swallow. The British, Japanese, and U.S. militaries employed this technique in the South Pacific during World War II, and even today it's used as a stopgap in places like the Solomon Islands when supplies are scarce, according to California emergency-room doctors Darilyn and Troy Falck, who have done so, and saved lives with it. The setup is simple: Suspend coco-nut over patient, run transfusion tubing from coconut's eye to human's arm, insert IV needle, and let it flow. But go easy. Too much of the juice would be toxic, due to its high potassium content. A typical patient's limit? Four nuts per day, tops.

Q: After I've spent a day sailing, why can I still feel waves long after I come ashore?

—KAREN PAUTZ, LEXINGTON, KENTUCKY

A: The feeling you describe is known as mal de debarquement (MDD), and it usually lasts about 24 hours, though on rare occasions it can linger for months or even years. According to Dr. Bradley Marple, an otolaryngologist (that's ear-nose-and-throat doc to you) at the University of Texas Southwestern Medical Center at Dallas, the cause is still debated, but most doctors suspect that MDD is a temporary failure of the vestibular system. This network of fluid-filled ear canals is equipped with tiny motion-sensory receptors that tell the brain which direction you're moving. In the case of MDD, it seems, your vestibular system adapts to the motion experienced on a boat or small plane—constant rocking or swaying—and your brain takes a while to readjust once that stimulus is removed. This hypothesis remains unproven, but Marple says that scientists do know how to combat MDD: No matter how sea-legged you are, don't confine yourself to bed. "Get out and trudge around," he advises. "Your brain needs to be reprogrammed, and that's more likely to happen if you're putting it through a workout."

Q: When cyclists draft each other, does the drafting cause drag on the leader?

—ED REIFF, SKOKIE, ILLINOIS

A: Actually, everybody benefits from drafting—the lead rider just benefits less. It's well known that the leader, by cutting wind resistance, makes life smoother for the rest of the pack—at race speeds, 17 percent easier for the second rider, 38 percent for the next, and 40 percent for the fourth position on back. But the guy fronting the pace line doesn't do more work than he would if cycling by himself; in fact, he uses 3 percent less energy. According to Chester Kyle, a Long Beach, California–based aerodynamicist who's designed ultrasleek clothes for Lance Armstrong, a cyclist riding solo creates several drag-inducing vortices around him, as well as low-pressure cavities that suck him backwards. If there's a rider clinging to his back wheel, those anomalies in the slipstream straighten out. The same goes for freeway driving. Tailgaters, oddly enough, save you gas.

Q: Can humans live without sunlight?

—SAID SAILLANT, VIA E-MAIL

A: In theory, says George Brainard, a neuroscientist at Philadelphia's Thomas Jefferson University, you could live out your normal life span in a dark bunker—with some important caveats. Lacking sunlight or artificial light, your circadian rhythms would get out of whack, greatly reducing your capacity for quality sleep and making you no fun to be around. Getting night and day desynchronized is thought to double the risk of cardiovascular disease, which could shorten your life. So could cancer, which might result from a lack of vitamin D, an essential nutrient released when sunlight hits your skin. More to the point, without massive vitamin D supplements or exposure to UV light, your muscles would turn to Jell-O within a year, and you'd be unable to take care of yourself. The moral: Always go toward the light.

. . . .

Q: We all know that Europeans brought deadly germs to the New World. Were the tables ever turned?

—KRIS ROMERO, THOUSAND OAKS, CALIFORNIA

A: Probably not, says Stephen Kunitz, professor of social and behavioral medicine at the University of Rochester. Most of humanity's big, bad epidemics developed in the

cities of Europe, crowded as they were with people and animals. (Measles likely originated in cattle, influenza in pigs,
etc.) Hundreds of generations of contact with those bugs
allowed the survivors to develop acquired immunities, a
luxury Native Americans didn't have. As a result, explains
evolutionary biologist Jared Diamond in his Pulitzer
Prize–winning *Guns, Germs, and Steel,* an estimated 95 percent of the New World's Indians died from disease within
150 years of 1492. Some scientists think that evidence of
syphilis in the Americas going back at least 800 years—
along with a European outbreak of that disease just after
Columbus's return—indicates it may have worked the
opposite way at least once. But recently discovered
syphilitic skeletons in Hull, England, possibly predating
Columbus, have cast this theory into doubt.

•   •   •   •   •   •   •   •

Q: Where does the white go when the snow melts?

—*Joe Schmitz, St. Paul, Minnesota*

A: Not to get too Zen on you, Joe-dude, but there isn't any
white, so it doesn't go anywhere. To understand why snow
looks white, consider an ice cube: You look at it from some
angles, and it's transparent. From other angles it shines,
which means it's reflecting light. Now, snow consists of zil-
lions of minuscule ice crystals, and each one of them acts
like the cube, sometimes bouncing the light, sometimes let-

ting it through. But there are so many crystals, and they're so small and randomly heaped together, that ultimately almost all the light that hits the snow is scattered and reflected back. That's pretty much the definition of whiteness. All this, of course, applies to the "country" kind of snow. For urban slush, the question is where the gray goes, and the answer is simple: It's on my car, and you can come see for yourself anytime you like.

. . . .

Q. I heard that when bats exit their caves at night, they always turn to the left. Is this really true?

—STEVE SMITH, WEST CONSHOCKEN, PENNSYLVANIA

A. Negative, Batman. The nocturnal flying mammals often exit their caves flocking leftward, but that's by no means written in instinctual stone. Bats, which subsist on insects and fruit, are just like any fast-food-loving human—where they head to eat is determined by whims of their voracious appetites. "If they're looking for moths that hang out near the cotton fields, they'll make a beeline for the cotton fields," says Bob Benson, public information manager for Bat Conservation International, an Austin, Texas–based research facility that owns a cavern that's home to 20 million free-tailed bats. "The direction is determined by where their favorite foraging grounds are situated." But even though the direction isn't always left, it is predetermined.

YOUR BODY, THE BACKCOUNTRY

Usually a scout will venture from the cave early and return with a report on foraging conditions, delivered via ultrasonic vocalizations. After all, if every bat was driven randomly by its own palate, their mass exits could causes nightly 20-million-bat pileups.

Chapter 3

WHAT IN THE WORLD?

QUANDARIES ABOUT THE BLUE PLANET

Q: How come the five major whirlpools in the world—Corryvreckan, Old Sow, Moskstraumen, Saltstraumen, and Naruto— are all in the Northern Hemisphere?

—GEORGE HERRERA, POMPANO BEACH, FLORIDA

A: Indeed, the five tongue-twisting pools you mention all do swirl north of the equator, but their existence there is the result of either maritime history or a geographical fluke rather than the laws of hydrodynamics. Whirlpools, which can range from 30 to 300 feet across, occur when a fast current, usually driven by strong tides, is forced through a narrow fjord opening or a strait, or between two coastal islands, where it reacts with an opposing force— such as a current from a river mouth or a sharp turn in an undersea channel—that alters its course. As the current gets shoved upward and pushed in another direction, it begins to spiral around the turbulence, forming a vortex. The requisite conditions (strong tides, narrow landmasses, and river mouths) are by no means exclusive to the Northern Hemisphere. In fact, according to David Frantantoni, an oceanographer at the Woods Hole Oceanographic Institute, in Massachusetts, similar-sized vortexes exist south of the equator, but the five "major" whirlpools you've listed are simply better known. Why? For centuries, the vast majority of world shipping took place in the Northern Hemisphere, and thanks to harrowing real-life incidents and a few tall tales, these pools gained notoriety for the threat they posed to the maritime industry. Other pools, such as those known to exist off the coast of New Zealand and near the Strait of Magellan, were never named because by the time they were discovered they no longer posed a significant threat to the modern shipping industry's motorized vessels. Hey, nobody ever said fame was fair.

* * * * * * * *

Q: What is the most common tree?

—NEIL HARRISON, REED CITY, MICHIGAN

A: You might assume the most ubiquitous tree would be a rainforest specimen, but it's not so. Those sweaty jungles are a crowded mosaic of different species. Peter Lee, a biologist at Global Forest Watch Canada, says that the John Smith of trees is the Siberian larch, numbering in the high hundreds of millions in the forests of eastern Russia, Siberia, and northern China. While no one has done a full count, this deciduous conifer's wide distribution in Russia's boreal (northern) forests, which are three times the size of North America's, places it ahead of two runners-up, the black spruce of Canada and Russia's Siberian spruce. For both the long-lived larch and the spindly but hardy spruce, an effective propagator, global warming is a serious concern. As temperatures rise, their range will be pushed farther north and they'll become more susceptible to fire. Both factors could devastate the boreal forests and, as with the rainforests, the results would be unpleasant for, well, all life on Earth.

QUANDARIES ABOUT THE BLUE PLANET

Q: If the purpose of berries is to be eaten by animals, which then scatter the seeds so the plant can reproduce, then why are there poisonous berries?

—ROSALIE POTTS, WAYNE, MAINE

A: The assumption here is that berries exist to be eaten by animals and dispersed in their poop. Unfortunately, this is flawed on two counts. First, the chief purpose of berries, like all fruit, is to protect the seed—think of them as nature's bubble wrap—until the plant is ready to propagate new seedlings. Second, the seeds that get eaten are quite often digested, not excreted, which can spell reproductive trouble for the unlucky plant. "It's spending all its energy making seeds but isn't getting the return on its investment because its seeds are being gobbled up," says Kristina Schierenbeck, an evolutionary botanist at California State University at Chico. That's when the species needs to try another evolutionary strategy. It could develop a seed with a protective coating, which can pass through an animal's system and survive to germinate elsewhere, or it might lace its berries with poison. Animals will either snack on them and die, she says, or— like the bird that wisely spits out the toxic seeds when eating the fruit from a yew plant—learn a healthier behavior. Mind you, the same plants are not poisonous to

YECHH!

all animals, which complicates matters. So just because you see a rabbit gorging itself on death-cap mushrooms (*Amanita phalloides*), don't assume you can do the same. Then again, the words "death cap" probably tipped you off to that.

•　•　•　•　•　•　•　•

Why do some plants survive winter and some die?

—LEO ROOP, TUCSON, ARIZONA

A: The cold truth: Most plant cells rupture when jagged ice crystals form inside them, and if enough damage takes place, plants die. Of course, annual species, like geraniums and impatiens, are *supposed* to croak every year after dropping their seeds. For perennials, various strategies come into play. According to Chris Andersen, a plant physiologist at the Environmental Protection Agency (EPA), grasses produce antifreeze-like compounds made of sugar and proteins to lower the freezing point inside their cells. Woody-stemmed flowers like lilacs, shrubs such as rhododendrons, and most fruit trees rely on "extracellular freezing," winterizing themselves as the days get shorter by slowly dehydrating their most vital cells, thus forcing any ice to form outside those cells. And conifers protect trunks and branches the same way; plus, they grow sappy needles with low moisture content. Such plants aren't just hardy. They're chill.

Q: Which plant can survive at the highest elevation?

—*JASON SCHOENER, GRAND BLANC, MICHIGAN*

A: New species are discovered at higher sites every year, but the current altitude champ is a beige lichen found at 24,300 feet on Mount Everest's neighbor, Makalu. However, some people, explains biologist Stephan Halloy, of the New Zealand Institute for Crop & Food Research, don't count lichens as plants—they're the result of a symbiotic relationship between a fungus and an alga. Among vascular plants—which transport water to their leaves—the winner is *Saussurea gnaphalodes*, a low, hairy rosette that grows at up to 21,000 feet on Everest. It's no surprise the plant is runty: To survive at such heights, where CO_2 is scarce, alpine flora have to develop more stomata (the leaf pores that enhance gas exchange), hunker down, and invest more biomass in their roots than their shoots. When they're successful, says Halloy, high-altitude plants "can live up to three thousand years, rivaling the oldest known specimens on Earth. These plants are built to last."

•   •   •   •   •   •   •   •

Q: Do any of our household vegetables still grow in the wild?

—*MIKE PITASSI, RANCHO CUCAMONGA, CALIFORNIA*

A: Modern veggies are the result of thousands of years of artificial selection, which humans practiced in the old days by replanting the seeds they liked best and, in the past two hundred years, through horticulture and genetic tinkering. Most produce today has an ancestor that still exists in nature, but aside from a few wild potatoes and onions, nothing you find out there will resemble your tabletop carrots and celery. Take the wild cabbage (*Brassica olerace*), which still grows along the Mediterranean. About 2,500 years ago, says Frank Mangan, a horticulturist at the University of Massachusetts, the Greeks developed this foul little weed into the thing we now call cabbage. By the first century, the Romans had engineered it into kale and collard greens. A preference for the cabbage's immature flower buds led to the breeding of cauliflower, broccoli, and, in the 18th century, Brussels sprouts. As any kid will attest, you just can't get away from the stuff.

*   *   *   *   *   *   *

Q: If you're lost in the wild with a cell phone, can you get a clearer signal on high ground?

—NICK KOLIAS, SEATTLE, WASHINGTON

A: We'll assume that you're already aware of the limits of your cell phone as a backcountry rescue beacon. Despite the optimism of the "Can you hear me now?" guy, only 65 percent of the U.S. landmass is covered by cellular service. That said, your phone's signals, like an FM radio's, travel in a straight line, so even though they can bounce off solid objects—like mountains—and reach you in low-lying areas, the solid objects don't always cooperate. That's when climbing to higher ground may get you in the line of sight of a tower, if there's one fairly close. You could also heed the advice of Verizon Wireless spokeswoman Andrea Linskey: While hiking, occasionally look down at your handset to note where you get a good signal. If you need to make an emergency call, turn around, and be thankful you left those breadcrumbs.

Q: Why do we float better in salty water than in fresh water?

—*Maureen Purvis, Greenville, North Carolina*

A: It all comes down to a concept known as specific gravity, a measure of density that's determined by the ratio of the weight of a given volume of a substance to that of an equal volume of another substance—usually pure water. Simply put, if an object has a specific gravity less than that of a fluid, it will float on that fluid. Since humans are largely water, your specific gravity weighs in right around that of pure water, measured at 1.0, and you either barely float or barely sink. The dissolved minerals in salt water, on the other hand, boost its specific gravity to at least 1.02. So, if you swam in the notoriously saline Dead Sea, you'd float better—some 50 percent higher (with three-quarters of your body out of the water) than you would on Lake Michigan. Climb into a bathtub of chocolate pudding and you'd float like an air mattress. We'll spare you the complicated physics—involving Archimedes' Principle (why and how buoyancy force makes us float)—but to understand it intuitively, take up windsurfing: Shortboards that float on the ocean can feel like sinkers on a lake. *(Contributed by Stephanie Pearson)*

* * * * * * * *

Q: How do mountaineers decide where base camp goes?

—BILL LEE, TROY, NEW YORK

A: There's no decree from on high regarding where base camp should be located, says Seattle-based climbing guide Eric Simonson. Nor is it stated that every mountain has to have one. But when it comes to the big peaks like those in the Himalayas, "BC" is usually established, he says, simply "at the end of the road," the point beyond which you have to stop relying on trucks, animals, and porters and start climbing. It needs to be low enough—generally below 15,000 feet—for climbers who are sick or tired to go there to recover, yet not so low that starting back up takes too long.

If you're looking for an appropriate site, you'll want it to have sunshine, flat ground, and clean water nearby, plus protection from wind, avalanches, and rockfall. Not surprisingly, the BC on Everest's south side is considered one of the world's most forbidding. According to American climber Ed Viesturs, this legendary camp, on the moraine of the Khumbu Glacier at over 17,500 feet, is so high that recuperation is difficult. So what's the cushiest? At a mere 13,369 feet, the base camp on Pakistan's 26,660-foot Nanga Parbat is composed of a sunny, grassy moraine with a peaceful stream and oodles of wildflowers—what Viesturs fondly calls "supreme flip-flops-and-shorts territory."

Why don't we get thunder and lightning during winter storms?

—GREG STEINACKER, AUGUSTA, WISCONSIN

A: For lightning to occur in winter—as in summer—relatively warm air must clash with cold air, and the lighter, warmer air must rise 30,000 to 45,000 feet into the upper troposphere. Ripe conditions might occur on a cool afternoon in February when an extremely cold low-pressure system moves in, lifting the cool air heavenward. On the way up, those warm water molecules rub elbows with cold molecules in a cloud, causing all the molecules to shed electrons, which collect at the bottom of the cloud. When enough electrons are buzzing around the base, they're attracted to the ground (which temporarily has an opposite charge). Then *kaboom!* Lightning streaks to the earth, breaking the sound barrier and creating thunder. In the U.S., winter lightning happens most often in the Southeast when extremely cold low-pressure systems move through and collide with the warmer air ahead. It also happens on the coasts, when an inland cold front butts up against warmer sea breezes. "I suppose any cold front is a potential lightning producer," says UCLA staff meteorologist James Murakami. "But to really get cooking, you got to have heat."

. . . .

Q: Do lakes really die? I heard several years back that Lake Titicaca had died. If so, how and why?

—OLETA LONGMIRE, BIG CABIN, OKLAHOMA

A: The term "dead lake" is misleading. Often it's used to describe a lake that has suffered a major fish kill because of acid rain. But while those particular fish are gone forever, a dead lake can eventually be brought back to life by adding massive amounts of lime to neutralize the acid. Ironically, in other instances, a dead lake can actually have too much life. When agricultural fertilizers drain into a lake, algae fed by the nitrogen and phosphorous bloom in such huge quantities that they smother the fish. Thankfully, 3-million-year-old Titicaca is still alive, despite having had a tough go of it during the last several decades. In the early 1940s, at Peru's request, the U.S. Fish and Wildlife Service stocked its 3,200 square miles with common North American rainbow trout, believing they would help feed locals living along the shore. But the plan backfired when the hungry trout nearly eradicated two native fish species, the boga and the humanto. Tourist accommodations along the lakeshore, many of which allow raw sewage and chemicals to drain directly into the water, haven't helped either. But, says Ben Orlove, author of *Lines in the Water: Nature and Culture at Lake Titicaca,* "Compared to other ancient lakes, Titicaca is in pretty good shape."

* * * * * * * *

Q: Could you please explain to me how a propane lantern makes light. I studied those mantles in many an ice hut for years. How's it done?

—MATT PETERSON, WASHINGTON, D.C

A: First, a little Thermodynamics 101. Back in 1901, an aging German physicist named Max Planck made a brilliant discovery. He found that any atom, when sufficiently heated, ejects electrons and—to remain balanced—subsequently releases photons, which are energy in the form of heat and light. Planck recognized that different elements give off light at different temperatures and that certain substances give off more light than others, which is where the lantern comes in. The lantern's mantle, a small woven bag that acts as a wick, is a blend of magnesium, cerium, and the rare-earth metal yttrium. Pump propane vapor into the chamber surrounding the mantle, put a match to the mantle, and the magnesium and cerium ignite like kindling. But to get that familiar yellow light, you have to increase the flow of gas and oxygen so the propane and mantle burn hotter. At temperatures between 1,000 and 2,000 degrees Fahrenheit, yttrium burns brighter than any other metal, shedding photons like a dog shaking off water and burning only minimal gas. It's an elegantly simple design often taken for granted, it seems, unless you're a man sitting in an ice hut for a really long time.

*　　*　　*　　*　　*　　*　　*　　*

On a hiking trip in Yosemite, our reward was the roaring Nevada Falls. We sat and stared at the rush and soaked in the fine mist. But some five minutes later, when we finally looked away from the falls, the valley walls suddenly appeared to stretch like Play-Doh—not just to me, but to everyone in the group. Was it something in the water, or what?

—CLAY CARTER, SUNSET BEACH, CALIFORNIA

A: Don't panic—sounds like you were simply experiencing "motion after-effect," a.k.a. the waterfall illusion. First noted by Aristotle around 350 B.C. and later documented in 1834 by English philosopher Robert Addams—who experi-

QUANDARIES ABOUT THE BLUE PLANET

enced the phenomenon while viewing a cascade in Foyers, Scotland—this psychedelic illusion occurs after prolonged viewing of any uniformly moving surface, be it a waterfall or a Tour de France peleton. The reason? Inside your gray matter are thousands of specialized brain cells that sense motion. Some of these neurons detect downward activity, some perceive left-to-right movement (or vice versa), and still others sense upward motion. When you focus on a waterfall, downward-sensing cortical neurons become over-stimulated and fatigued, throwing your entire motion-detection system out of balance. Consequently, when you avert your gaze, the exceptionally vibrant remaining neurons go into overdrive, and stationary objects seem to scroll upward or stretch like a Salvador Dalí clock. But as you probably noted, there's no permanent effect—you can go ahead and stare at waterfalls as long as you like. The illusion, which can last anywhere from five to 30 seconds, subsides as soon as your downward neurons have had a chance to take a brief siesta.

•   •   •   •   •   •   •   •

Q: Why does campfire smoke always seem to drift toward me?

—DUSTIN RODGERS, PAYSON, ARIZONA

A: You might say smoke follows beauty, but—no offense—it's probably one of two more plausible explanations. Fire scientists believe this unpleasant natural phenomenon is just an

illusion, created by swirling wind. "It's a roulette wheel, and it just feels like you're always the loser no matter where you sit," postulates Stephen Pyne, author of 10 books on fire, including *Fire: A Brief History*. BLM smoke management specialist Carl Gossard, on the other hand, attributes it to a crueler irony: Sit with your back to the wind to avoid the smoke and you actually force the breeze to eddy around you, pick up those pernicious fumes, and blow them in your face. Whichever theory you subscribe to, be aware of diurnal changes in the wind. "During the day, canyon breezes blow uphill, but at night they blow downhill," says Gossard. And on the beach, wind tends to blow onshore during the day, and offshore at night. "So if you're sitting around the fire for a really long time, you're going to have to make an adjustment." Suck it up, switch seats, or try yelling, "I hate rabbits!" three times in a row. Even if it's not a permanent solution, screaming anything will blow the smoke away for a moment.

Q: Is it true that when you get to a certain point near the North or South Pole, your compass stops working?

—*Tony Marzo, Copper Mountain, Colorado*

A: Yes. Above the Arctic Circle and below the Antarctic Circle, compasses will deviate by as much as 180 degrees from true north. That is because the magnetic poles are about a thousand miles from the true poles. But that's not a compass's only problem. Polar explorer Robert Peary reported after his 1891–1892 trip to the Arctic that his compass acted very "sluggish" and didn't always point north. When he sailed over the magnetic pole the source of magnetic attraction was directly beneath him, so rather than spinning north or south, the needle dipped downward. Explorers like Peary employed a variety of tools and techniques to chart their progress, including dead reckoning and a sextant, a device that measures latitude and longitude using celestial objects. Should you visit Nunavut or Tuktoyaktuk nowadays, you might want to bring a GPS and let satellites be your guide.

Q: Taking into consideration the movement of the heavens and Earth, how fast am I going if I'm standing still on the equator?

—MARK BENALLACK, MUSKEGON, MICHIGAN

A: It's a matter of perspective. To someone standing next to you at zero degrees latitude, you'd appear stationary. To a Martian hovering over the Earth, you'd appear to be spinning at 1,041 miles per hour. Icarus, looking back at you from the sun, would see that in addition to riding the terrestrial Tilt-A-Whirl, you are orbiting the home star at approximately 60,641 mph. From an outpost on the edge of Andromeda Galaxy, the Earth would be seen spinning, orbiting, and finally spiraling through the Milky Way, at an average speed of 584,601 mph. Add this all up and you are traveling at a top speed of 646,283 mph. But not so fast—the universe itself is expanding, at an immeasurable rate, so it is ultimately impossible to quantify how fast we're really going. "You'd need a reference point outside the universe," notes Mike Kobrick, a researcher at NASA's Jet Propulsion Laboratory in Pasadena, California. "I'm talking about higher dimensional space. I know I don't have that kind of perspective." Think you do? Please don't write us.

What is the oldest river in the world?

—*KENT WOSEPKA, HAMILTON, MASSACHUSETTS*

A: That's a tough one, because it's hard to determine whether any river today is the same river that was there 10 million years ago. Given that, many scientists cite the Finke River, in central Australia, as the most ancient. Vic Baker, a paleohydrologist at the University of Arizona in Tucson, says that while this is far from verifiable, the Finke is definitely very old. The reason: It runs in a line perpendicular to the local geological structure—in this case, a couple of mountain ranges—an indication that the river was present before the structure formed. As the mountains pushed up, the river cut deep canyons, the rimrock of which shows 400 million years of erosion. Since it can be presumed that this rock was once at river level, the river must be at least 400 million years old. Mind you, as with other "world's oldest rivers," most interest in the topic comes not from scientists but from local tourist boards. "I guess it sounds sexy," Baker speculates, "to say your town has the oldest river."

Q: Why is there a "hole" in the Continental Divide in Wyoming, and where does rain that falls there end up?

—*Dean Land, Portland, Oregon*

A: When the Continental Divide—the spine of North and South America, which separates rivers that ultimately flow to the Atlantic from those flowing to the Pacific—reaches southern Wyoming, it splits in two and encircles a 4,000-square-mile depression called the Great Divide Basin. According to Arthur Snoke, a geology professor at the University of Wyoming, in Laramie, the basin was formed starting around 65 million years ago, when the faulting and folding that created the eastern Rockies caused an uplift on all sides of this piece of land, cutting it off from the watershed. Thus, all the rain that falls in the basin, which on average is 500 feet lower than the ridges surrounding it, either ends up in the basin's groundwater or evaporates. This isn't the only unusual water feature on the divide. Just south of Yellowstone National Park, a stream on the western side of the divide called North Two Ocean Creek becomes the victim of "stream piracy." Atlantic Creek, on the eastern side of the same ridge, is slowly extending its gully uphill through erosion, and it now, in effect, crosses the divide and captures some of Two Ocean Creek, while the rest of Two Ocean continues west, under the moniker Pacific Creek. Which makes this point the Parting of the Waters landmark, the only place in this country where you can swim in water that's bound for two seas.

Q: **My son read an adventure book called *Brian's Winter,* in which it gets so cold that trees explode. Does that really happen?**

—*KARYN KAY, NEW YORK, NEW YORK*

A: In Gary Paulsen's 1996 novel about the harrowing exploits of 13-year-old Brian Robinson—who survives a winter in the Canadian woods by overcoming a bear attack, a shortage of grub, and biting cold—the title character wakes up one morning to find trees cracking like rifles and sending foot-long splinters his way. Exciting though it is, that's a stretch. Oregon State University plant physiologist Les Fuchigami says trees do split open suddenly, but not in the morning, and not this dramatically. The phenomenon is called frost cracking, and it can happen to hardwoods that have wounds in their bark. It occurs late in the day, after the sun has warmed the tree and then receded behind a cloud or set, causing the air temperature to plunge and cooling the outside of the tree too quickly. The temperature shift creates mechanical stress inside the tree, leading to . . . well, not really a bang, but a loud whimper.

Q: If you can't compost, is it more ecologically sound to put food down the garbage disposal or send it to the landfill?

—*Peter Keppler, Watertown, Massachusetts*

A: It depends on what the local waste-processing plant does with your crud, says Jeremy O'Brien, a North Carolina–based engineer with the Solid Waste Association of North America. If you put your waste down the disposal, it flows, along with household sewage, to a plant where it gets separated into thick sludge and treated wastewater. The sludge is placed in tanks and heated until anaerobic bacteria consume all the organic materials in it. This produces methane, a gas that some facilities turn into electricity to run their operations. Many plants also sell the dried sludge cakes as fertilizer or use them for fuel. If your plant puts sludge to use in one of these ways, stuff that grub down the disposal— it's more earth-friendly than having it hauled away by a diesel truck. But if it still sends sludge to the dump, you're better off saving the plant (and those hardworking bacteria) all that energy by trashing it yourself.

Q: How much does Mount Everest weigh?

—J. JOSHUA PLACA, SEDONA, ARIZONA

A: You pose an interesting question, Grasshopper, but one fraught with many dangerous curves. For starters: What is Mount Everest? "Does it start at Base Camp, at 17,500 feet?" asks Roger Bilham, a geophysics professor at the University of Colorado, "or 25 miles lower, in the Earth's crust? Or somewhere in between?" For the sake of this exercise, let's go with Base Camp. Our next challenge is determining the density of the rock. While the 29,035-foot-high summit is mostly limestone—and clays and silts make up the section at about 26,000 feet that climbers call the Yellow Band—the rest of the mountain is basically a big hunk of granite and gneiss, rocks with densities of about 170 pounds per cubic foot. Calculating the mountain's volume in cubic feet is trickier. Since Everest is more or less a cone, and a cone's volume is one-third of the base area times the height, we need to find the base area. To do so, square the radius—which averages out to 2.5 miles—and multiply that by π to get an answer of 547 million square feet. Going with our height of roughly 11,500 feet from Base Camp to summit, we can peg the volume at 2.1 trillion cubic feet. Multiply that by the density and, eureka! Everest tips the scale at a honking 357 trillion pounds. And then there's the snow and ice.

Q: What place on Earth is the farthest from land?

—MIKE MCNEILLY, PORTSMOUTH, NEW HAMPSHIRE

A: Like many escapists before you, the locale you seek is Point Nemo, a watery coordinate in the South Pacific so dubbed by Hrvoje Lukatela, of the Calgary, Alberta, software company Geodyssey Limited. To pinpoint Nemo (named for the headstrong captain in Jules Verne's *20,000 Leagues Under the Sea*), Lukatela input some 10 million map points into the company's Hipparchus program and "found the one whose distance to the closest point on land is the maximum." That spot turns out to be 48°52'32" south, 123°23'33" west—or exactly 1,670 miles from each of three landfalls: Maher Island, off the coast of Antarctica; Ducie Island, 325 miles east of Pitcairn Island; and Motu Nui, right next door to Chile's Easter Island.

. . . .

Q: Why does water expand as it cools, while everything else seems to contract?

—LINCOLN BLEVEANS, PAWLING, NEW YORK

A: Actually, water does contract until it gets down to about 39 degrees Fahrenheit. Like most matter, it's composed of molecules that move more slowly as heat is removed, causing the spaces between them to shrink. But water's a little funky. As the temperature approaches the freezing point,

QUANDARIES ABOUT THE BLUE PLANET

says John Chen, an applied scientist at Dartmouth, H_2O molecules rearrange themselves in 3-D structures called lattices—series of six-sided rings of molecules connected by hydrogen bonding. Because water molecules can bond only at certain angles, these lattices are full of empty space, and the solid takes up more room than the liquid. The result? Your ice tray overfloweth.

* * * * * * * *

How steep can a mountain get before it becomes unstable?

—ROBERT KEIL, LOS ANGELES, CALIFORNIA

A: If the conditions are right, any slope can succumb to a landslide—even surfaces that are practically horizontal. The general rule of thumb is this: If the angle of an unconsolidated slope is greater than the angle of repose (defined as the maximum angle at which loose material—say, sand or rock debris—will remain in place without sliding), the slope is in danger of failing. Sand, for instance, has an angle of repose of roughly 34 degrees, so if a windstorm whips a dune into a 45-degree precipice, chances are it'll slide. The rules change, however, in the presence of one or more "landslide initiation processes," a blanket term for factors that act to decrease the static friction that holds loose material together. These include rapid snowmelt, water-level changes, volcanic eruptions, earthquakes, and excessive rainfall. Burned areas, which are stripped of vegetation and have chemically altered soil that's more vulnerable to water saturation, and hillsides with distinct layers—clay on top of volcanic soil, for example—can also be prone to sliding, regardless of the slope's angle. But there's no way to tell by eyeballing it, so consult a U.S. Geological Survey hazard map, which identifies landslide danger zones, before your next scramble up a talus face. A last resort, says Lynn Highland, a geographer with the USGS, is to use your ears: "If you hear a loud rumble coming down the canyon, it's time to get out of there."

*   *   *   *   *   *   *   *

Q **With so many species dying off due to habitat destruction, are new species being born?**

—*Trey Johnson, Washington, D.C.*

A: "Evolution never stops," says Eric Dinerstein, a biologist with the World Wildlife Fund. Even as some 30,000 species disappear each year (counting only those visible to the naked eye), new ones are always in the works. But that's the only good news. Since a new species takes, say, 100,000 years to emerge, scientists guess that the world's rate of

QUANDARIES ABOUT THE BLUE PLANET

extinction is now a million times greater than its rate of spe-
ciation. The bulk of this loss of life can be blamed on human
encroachment. In the 20th century, about 250,000 species
went missing, and as deforestation continues at an exponen-
tial clip, scientists fear that 25 to 50 percent of the 10 million
species among us could be gone in 100 years. Finally, as ecologically important creatures are getting the ax, just what
sorts of new species are coming onto the scene? Mostly
viruses, and a new mosquito that's said to be breeding in
the London Underground.

*   *   *   *   *   *   *   *   *

How fast would you have to fly a plane to keep a perpetual sunset before your eyes?

—*JEFF BECK, NEW ORLEANS, LOUISIANA*

A: Looking to prolong the cocktail hour, eh? To keep the
sun on the western horizon, you have to fly as fast as the
Earth is rotating at your latitude. Sunset chasers at the equator can simply divide the circumference of the Earth—24,902
miles—by 24 hours to find their answer: 1,038 miles per hour.
As you move to higher latitudes, the surface's rotation speed
drops. In your case, at 30 degrees north latitude in N'Awlins
(where the circumference is 21,600 miles), your eternal-
propulsion craft would need to go about 900 mph, or 1.4
times the speed of sound. Now that the 1,350-mph Concorde
is retired, there are no commercial flights moving at such

speeds—and, no, we don't recommend stealing an F-22. So head farther north. A 747 traveling from Oslo to Anchorage at the 60th parallel (circumference of 12,450 miles) would have to fly only 520 mph, well within its cruising speed of 570 mph. Another option: Take a trip to the North Pole in the fall. There, you can watch the sunset from the relative comfort of your igloo for about 30 days straight.

Q: What town is farthest from a McDonald's in the contiguous U.S.?

—ANONYMOUS

A: The Wild File's Hamburglar-like research team did some snooping and arrived at Glad Valley, South Dakota, on the Cheyenne River Indian Reservation. As the crow flies, Glad Valley is 99 miles northwest of the nearest McDonald's, in Pierre, South Dakota. The Mount Rushmore State also has the most special-sauce-free town as defined by driving distance: Bison, 154 miles from the closest franchise, in Sturgis. Meanwhile, for nature lovers who also love Ronald, the most McDonald's-friendly national park is Yellowstone, a long McNugget's throw from a Happy Meal in West Yellowstone, Montana.

Q: Has anyone ever used a seat cushion as a flotation device?

—*ANONYMOUS*

A: Yes, in at least two cases, those butt savers have probably really saved butts. In 1978, when an Antilles Air Boat went down near the U.S. Virgin Islands, survivors grabbed onto cushions that had popped free; and after the aborted 1989 takeoff of a USAir 737 at LaGuardia Airport, flight attendants tossed seat bottoms to passengers in the chilly water, some of whom couldn't swim. Seats are allowed as flotation devices only on inland flights; as National Transportation Safety Board investigator Mark George explains, the FAA requires planes with extended over-water routes to carry more buoyant life preservers and inflatable rafts. But those devices take time to prepare, and time is scarce in plane ditchings. Maybe that's why flight attendants on Southwest Airlines end their safety briefing with this tip: "In the event of a water landing, please take your seat cushion with you as a complimentary gift."

Q: Can a river flow uphill?

—*MARSHALL PERRY, SAN FRANCISCO, CALIFORNIA*

A: Gravity and other forces dictate that the overall course of a river is always from higher to lower, but water can run into conditions where it has nowhere to go but up. Scientists point to a giant scour hole in the Columbia River in Washington as evidence that catastrophic flooding during the last ice age made the extremely high river flow uphill for thousands of feet to escape the trough it was in. In our milder era, this happens only in limited stretches, but there are plenty of rivers that are known to reverse direction from time to time. In the case of a tidal bore, like the one in Canada's Bay of Fundy, a strong rising tide can enter a river channel and push the water back upstream. And hydrometeorologist Jonathan J. Gourley, of the National Severe Storms Laboratory, in Norman, Oklahoma, says a localized downpour can cause sections of a river to be higher downstream than upstream, which sends the water back the way it came. But in the end, all that liquid must go with the flow.

Q: Where do human beings live the longest lives, and what's their secret?

—GEORGE CHIU, WALNUT CREEK, CALIFORNIA

A: For centuries there have been tales of longevity-boosting Shangri-Las—like the Hunza region of Pakistan, the Vilcabamba area in Ecuador, and Georgia's Caucasus Mountains—where people live to 130 or 140. Sadly, these appear to be myths, perhaps attempts to bring some areas renown and/or tourist dollars. But if the Fountain of Youth doesn't exist, there are places where people have a higher chance of reaching 100. According to Boston University's Tom Perls, a medical expert on aging, the top three are the Japanese island of Okinawa, Nova Scotia, and Sardinia. Scientists can't explain why these areas spawn healthier oldsters, but it may have to do with a more active, agrarian lifestyle, a diet rich in fish, and lower daily calorie counts. Still, you never know. The longest documented human life belonged to a woman from a country where diets are rich in richness: France's own Jeanne Louise Calment, who expired in 1997 at age 122.

Q: What ski area is closest to the equator, and how good is the snow?

—JOHN PIERSON, WAYZATA, MINNESOTA

A: You can backcountry ski practically right on the equator—in Ecuador and on Africa's Mount Kenya—but the closest ski area is 1,100 miles away in Bolivia, at a sketchy nonresort called Chacaltaya. It lies at 16 degrees south latitude in the Cordillera Real, on a glacier at a jaw-dropping 17,785 feet—also making it the highest ski area in the world. If you think skiing even a bunny hill at that elevation would take the lungs of Ed Viesturs, you're right; thankfully, Chacaltaya's single run is only about 300 feet long. But there's no guarantee you'll see any snow, and the glacier is melting fast. In short, Vail it ain't. The hill is open only one day a week (Sunday), and admission is $8. It also doesn't hurt to bring fuel to help run the cable tow, which people fall off all the time, according to Javier Thellaeche, of outfitter Andean Summits. "Then everyone else falls as well." By the time you make the top, he says, "you're so tired you don't want to ski."

Q: Who answers 911 calls made on a satellite phone?

—DAVID LANGSTON, HARRISBURG, PENNSYLVANIA

A: Unless you're a Globalstar customer, dialing 911 from a sat phone will get you nothing but silence. There's no emergency number that works all over the globe, and dialing zero won't get you an English operator. So play it smart: Bring the number of a local rescue authority, and have a contact you can reach at home who knows how to get through to the locals. (As Everest guide Eric Simonson notes, calls from the Himalayas to the U.S. are often clearer than calls within the country.) Better yet, subscribe to a private emergency service like International SOS ($245 a year); they speak English and can set up a rescue with local services. But before you reach for the handset—and this goes for cell users, too—be sure you've tried every alternative and that you're truly in a fix. You may be asking people to risk their lives to save yours.

Q: Was the interstate highway system designed so that 1 in every 5 miles is straight enough to be a runway in times of war or emergency?

—Anonymous

A: Fortunately for you nervous drivers, no. This urban legend seems to date from the early 1940s, when the Army Air Force and the Public Roads Administration, with war on the horizon, started building airstrips adjacent to public highways. Only 26 were completed, and the Eisenhower Interstate System of 1956 included nothing about airstrips or any one-in-five rule. Of course, that doesn't stop dozens of pilots a year from using the interstates as their own personal landing strips. This past May, a traffic plane from a San Francisco news channel ran out of fuel and had to plunk down on the East Bay Freeway. In this case, no harm was done—aside from some traffic snarls, as seen on other stations.

* * * * * * * * *

Q: What's the difference between talus and scree?

—Mike Mendonsa, Federal Way, Washington

A: These two words are often spoken in the same breath, and indeed, both are defined in the *Dictionary of Geological Terms* as "a heap of rock waste at the base of a cliff." An informal survey of climbers suggests that, for some, the words are interchangeable, while others feel that size matters. Scree is usually thought of as the gravel spread across a steep slope, while talus implies rocks that are fist-size, head-size, or even furniture-size. For climber-adventurer Will Gadd, the important part is whether you're going up the mountain or down: "Talus means boulders—period. Scree is the slippery stuff that, on the ascent, causes you to fall on your ass. But on the descent it's beauteous, because you can slide down it like a skier." So just remember: *Scree* rhymes with *whee!*

•   •   •   •   •   •   •   •   •

Q: Will the Earth's interior ever cool off completely?

—*J. T. Leeson, Franklin, Tennessee*

A: Yes, but probably not before the sun becomes a red giant and swallows our planet, about 10 billion years from now. In the meantime, things will get gnarly here on Earth Island. According to Paul Asimow, a professor of geology and geochemistry at the California Institute of Technology, the Earth's outer core—a layer of liquid iron surrounding the solid inner core—is cooling and solidifying every year. Since the dynamo effect caused by the core's movement gives the Earth its magnetic field, that field will eventually be gone. This is bad news for humans, because the field repels intense radiation from the sun that, if unimpeded, would cause skyrocketing cancer rates. Another dire consequence: The globe's upper mantle will cool and harden, making magma generation almost impossible, which in turn will lock up plate tectonics and put an end to volcanoes and earthquakes. That may sound good, but it's awful. Without these processes, new continental crust will stop forming and the continents will erode into the sea. Eventually, the entire Earth will be covered with water. "Yes, the news is ultimately bad," says Asimow, not so soothingly. "But you already knew that."

.   .   .   .

Q: **How did early explorers find the North Pole, when faced with 24-hour sunshine and a magnetic pole that was far from the geographical pole they sought?**

—CHRIS YEATS, TULSA, OKLAHOMA

A: You're correct to assume that a compass won't lead you to the top of the world, but you don't need constellations to guide you. T. H. Baughman, a polar historian at the University of Central Oklahoma, says that with just a sextant, a device called an artificial horizon, and astronomical tables, people 250 years ago had the requisite tools for tracking the sun to find latitude 90 north. But because polar conditions are tough on these sensitive instruments, the

QUANDARIES ABOUT THE BLUE PLANET

technique wasn't foolproof. In fact, it seems increasingly likely that American Robert Peary, long believed to be the first to the pole, in 1909, didn't make it. Small calculational errors probably had him off by a good 30 miles. It would be 1968 before American insurance salesman Ralph Plaisted finally became the first undisputed pole conqueror—as confirmed by an Air Force flyover.

. . . .

Q: Why does blowing on a flame extinguish it?

—ANONYMOUS

A: Eric Eddings, a chemical engineering professor at the University of Utah, says, "Flames are a product of a complex chemical reaction between a fuel source and oxygen in the air." When fuel, such as wood, is heated, its cellulose plant material breaks down and volatile gases are released. Once oxygen mixes with these gases, a spark will set it ablaze. When you blow gently on a fire, you put more O_2 into the equation and increase the rate of burning. Blow too hard and any of fire's three requisite elements can be removed: The fuel-oxygen mixture can get diluted (air is 78 percent nitrogen); the process can get cooled down too far; and the reaction can be removed from its fuel source (like when fire is blown away from a candle's wick). The result: Flame over.

When does a hill become a mountain?

—*Tony Soika, Neenah, Wisconsin*

A: You'll be happy to know that, if you're a taxpaying citizen, it's largely up to you. According to Lou Yost, chief of the Geographic Names Project at the U.S. Geological Survey, there's no official cutoff point. While the British have at times set firm standards for what constitutes a mountain, the American public can propose a name for any land feature by submitting it to the U.S. Board on Geographic Names. That body decides whether to accept the moniker based on two criteria: Is it in keeping with what the locals call it, and is it consistent with similar features in the area? For instance, if most of the protuberances around the hypothetical Mount J. Lo are called mountains, score a vote for "Mount." And vice versa. "Obviously," says Yost, "what people on the East Coast call a mountain might seem to someone in the West to be just a hill." In the end, it's usage that wins out. The highest spot in Ohio, 1,549-foot Campbell Hill, is taller than Mad River Mountain, a ski resort right next door.

QUANDARIES ABOUT THE BLUE PLANET

Q: What is the world's tallest iceberg?

—MARK GASPARD, TENNESSEE COLONY, TEXAS

A: Scientists obviously don't spend enough time rap-
pelling down icebergs with measuring tapes in hand,
because nobody knows. An iceberg's remoteness and constantly changing size make this a very elusive factoid. "But
we do know," offers Greg Rose, of the National Ice Center, a
government agency that tracks sea ice for commercial and
defense purposes, "the tallest iceberg ever officially recorded." That was an unnamed 1957 beauty spotted just off the
coast of Melville Bay, Greenland. From the surface up
(about seven-eighths of a berg remains hidden underwater),
it was 550 feet tall, or roughly one George short of the
Washington Monument.

Q: What would happen if the locks on the Panama Canal were destroyed?

—MIGUEL SALAZAR, IOWA PARK, TEXAS

A: Toward the end of World War II, the Japanese devised a plan to do just that, using bombers catapulted from enormous submarines. The war ended before the raid could be launched, but they had the right idea. The goal was to destroy the gates on either side of 166-square-mile Gatún Lake—the highest point of the canal, at 85 feet above sea level. According to Leo Cain, project manager at the U.S. Army Corps of Engineers, which built the canal in 1914, such an event would literally open the floodgates, sending 1.6 trillion gallons of water pouring out and overflowing the six 110-by-1,000-foot concrete locks. Any boats in the area would likely be demolished, and the lake's level would drop 50 feet. And because Gatún Lake is fed by the Chagres River, the water would keep flowing, turning the Panama Canal into Panama Falls and making it impassable to anything but the wiliest misdirected salmon.

QUANDARIES ABOUT THE BLUE PLANET

Q: What's the highest mountain that ever existed on Earth?

—LEIGH ANN ROBERTS, NASHVILLE, TENNESSEE

A: No one's sure, but according to Chuck Barnes, geology professor emeritus at Northern Arizona University, it's doubtful there's ever been a mountain much higher than ol' 29,035-foot Everest. Blame it on Archimedes' Principle: Mountains "float" on the Earth's slightly denser mantle just as a ship floats on water; add more height (meaning weight) and the mountain will sink farther into the mantle. On smaller planets, with less gravity, mountains are able to get taller—thus, a Sherpa on Mars would have to climb 80,000 vertical feet to summit Olympus Mons, the highest mountain in the solar system. Still, Barnes says, it's reasonable to think that our planet once hosted other mountains in the Everest ballpark. Evidence strongly suggests that 200 million years ago the Appalachians were similar in size to today's Himalayas.

* * * * * * * *

Q: What's the maximum number of people the Earth can hold?

—A. CIANCAGLINI, DENVER, COLORADO

A: We won't even begin to pretend there's a simple answer to this whopper of a question. Population projection is such a wildly unpredictable—and inherently political—conundrum that it's impossible to pin down an exact number. But that hasn't stopped some dauntless demographers from using computer modeling to variously estimate our planet's maximum occupancy, or "carrying capacity," to be between 7.7 billion and 12 billion people. World population over the last hundred years or so has exploded from 1.6 billion in 1900 to roughly 6 billion today. If present growth continues, we should easily hit this "no vacancy" ceiling within the next century. But before you settle into a deep Malthusian funk, consider a bright spot: 44 percent of the world's inhabitants now live in countries (such as Cuba and Thailand) where fertility is below replacement level. Even so, you don't have to be a deep-ecology alarmist to wonder: Is there enough soil, water, and air to keep 12 billion human hearts alive and beating? Population doomsayers and shrill Cassandras—who warn of a coming "demographic winter" marked by famines and epidemics—have been wrong before, and there are many optimists who still have faith that science and technology can provide the means to avert environmental catastrophe while keeping everyone fed. Maintaining a universally decent standard of living, however, is another story altogether, and some argue we've already exceeded carrying capacity without even realizing it.

Chapter 4

THE CARBON Factor

LIFE...NOTHING BUT LIFE

Q: Does the early bird really get the worm?

—*Jayne Mueller, Long Island, New York*

A: Yes, but the lazy lion gets the zebra. All animals are equipped with a biological clock that regulates basic bodily functions such as when they sleep, when they're most alert, etc. In humans (and most mammals), the clock is housed in the hypothalamus, a part of the brain just above the back of the throat that uses information gathered from the eyes to synchronize our bodies with the 24-hour day and releases important neurotransmitters like histamine, which signals us awake. Worms surface during the night and burrow back underground in the morning. Thus, a bird's clock triggers it to wake at dawn, before the slithery annelids retreat to safety. Lions and other cats, however, don't seem to be tightly controlled by a body clock. They'll steal the kill from a pack of wild dogs at night or stalk zebras in broad daylight. Their slothful reputation can be attributed to the African lions of the eastern Serengeti, which lie in wait along migratory routes because they know their dinner will likely walk right past them en route to water. "They're hardly lazy," says Barry Wakeman, retired director of education at the Cincinnati Zoo. "But smart? Yes."

Q: Does an animal feel more pain if it has a large brain?

—JOE FARAGO, DENVER, COLORADO

A: In other words, can you crush bugs without a guilt trip? Maybe. In order to feel the fatal *thwap* of a flyswatter, a critter needs special equipment like pain receptors, sensitive nerve fibers that send nerve impulses to the spinal cord and brain. While all fish, reptiles, amphibians, and mammals have pain receptors near their skin, some have more than others: Anglers can sleep a little easier knowing that a rainbow trout's mouth has fewer pain receptors than a dog's. But scientists are pretty clueless as to whether crustaceans, mollusks, and insects—with their small brains and unsophisticated nervous systems—feel true hurt. Take the common American lobster. Like all hard-shell invertebrates, it has no spinal cord, no pain receptors near the outside of its body, and no cerebral cortex (the area of the brain that translates pain impulses into the sensation of pain). Yet watch a lobster try to claw its way out of a pot of boiling water, and it's pretty obvious that the little guy is experiencing something. Exactly what, though, is hard to say. "We don't know if lobsters feel pain," says Edward Kravitz, a professor of neurobiology at Harvard Medical School, adding yet another disclaimer. "Since pain is a perception, we often don't know whether people feel it either."

" won't be late"

Dinner at 8.

Q: When dogs sniff each other, what are they smelling?

—*KIMBERLY BISHEFF, SANTA MONICA, CALIFORNIA*

A: A pooch who pokes its nose into the business end of another is sussing out a number of social cues. Dogs secrete pheromones, subtly smelly hydrocarbons, from many glands located in and around their genitals; these odors let others know if they're sniffing an old friend (dogs can recognize each other by smell after years of separation), and whether there's the possibility of mating (females in heat excrete pheromones so strong they can be detected blocks away). Most important, canines locate themselves in the dog hierarchy with a few sniffs. When approached by a dominant dog, a submissive pup will secrete from its anal glands the pungent scent of fear. We'll pass on trying to describe it and the potpourri of other canine olfactory signals, because—thankfully—for the most part, our noses aren't sensitive enough to detect them. "Dogs smell in technicolor, and we smell in black and white," says Stephen Zawistowski, an animal behaviorist with the American Society for the Prevention of Cruelty to Animals. "Trying to explain what a dog smells is like trying to describe a rainbow to a blind person."
(Contributed by Stephanie Pearson)

Q: Why do small birds sometimes relentlessly attack larger birds?

—D. Murray, Morris, Manitoba, Canada

A: Because birds, like all creatures, instinctively realize the power of "mobbing," as it's officially called. "Mobbing looks and sounds aggressive," says Sally Conyne, a research director with the National Audubon Society, "but it rarely leads to injury or death on either side of the brawl. Its main purpose, beyond saving the babies, is to teach the young to recognize the enemy for when they're grown-up birds entrusted with protecting the nest." Say a hungry crow casts an evil eye toward some grackle fledglings. It won't be long before the adult grackles shake their branches, calling attention to the interloper, and gather a posse to run it out of their territory. As soon as they flush the crow from the tree, the grackles launch a valiant aerial dogfight, swooping at it from behind and sometimes diving at its tail feathers and feet until it flees. The crow gets sweet revenge, in a way, when a hawk, eagle, owl, or, yes, human, trespasses on its territory: As many as 50 of its crow brethren will dive-bomb the invader until it leaves. Don't think that you're safe from harassment just because you've got a big brain and opposable thumbs, Conyne warns. Hitchcock's *The Birds* got it right.

Q: Do eels really migrate to the Sargasso Sea?

—DAVID MAAHS, ALBUQUERQUE, NEW MEXICO

A: Nearly all of the world's freshwater eels migrate to their ancestral homes in the ocean to spawn, but of the dozens of species out there, only the two North Atlantic ones—the American and the European eel—do it in the Sargasso, a 2-million-square-mile ellipse of glassy water that stretches southeast from Bermuda. Their larvae begin life in these famously weed-choked waters and travel hundreds or even thousands of miles to the rivers and lakes of North America and Europe. Eel specialist David Noakes, a professor of zoology at the University of Guelph, in Ontario, Canada, says the Sargasso, which is a warmwater eddy of the Gulf Stream, is ideally located to give the larvae, or leptocephali, a free ride to their freshwater stomping grounds—a trip that takes a year for American eels and up to three years for their Euro cousins. Once there, the slimy, snakelike fish live for 15 or 20 years, growing to lengths of between 3 and 5 feet. In the autumn of their lives, the eels return to the Sargasso to spawn—on the way they'll even slither onto wet ground to cross land barriers up to a mile long—and then die. "Being an eel is a tough way to make a living," Noakes says. "Next to the tuna, they're probably the hardest-working fish in the ocean."

Q: Do animals have a preference for the right or left paw?

—*NANCY GALLES, MANITOU SPRINGS, COLORADO*

A: This is an area of much debate in the dog-eat-dog world of animal psychology. But the evidence suggests that some animals favor one side for certain tasks—a phenomenon known as lateralization. For instance, a recent study found that toads with tape stuck to their backs usually used their right forepaw to get it off. Tool-wielding New Caledonian crows like to monitor with the right eye when manipulating objects in their claws, and humpback whales prefer to surface right side up when capturing prey. Lemurs, meanwhile, are usually lefties when it comes to grabbing their grub. Why do such preferences exist? According to biopsychologist William Hopkins, who studies lateralization in apes at Atlanta's Yerkes National Primate Research Center, "for animals and humans alike, the nervous system is more efficient if the two halves of the brain assume separate functions. If you want to peel a banana, you need one hand to hold the banana and the other to take the peel off. If both sides of the brain have to do both activities, you're not being very efficient." Witness the ambidextrous chimpanzee: In captivity, it typically picks branches up with its left hand but digs peanut butter out of a tube with its right. And when it comes to hurling feces at passersby, chimps that throw overhand tend to do so with the right hand, while underhanders switch from right to left. Go figure.

Q: I noticed a mockingbird and a robin mating near my house. What was that all about?

—JULIE HERNDON, YORKTOWN, VIRGINIA

A: Interspecies shagging, more commonly known as hybridization, is fairly widespread in the avian world—but it happens almost exclusively between birds of the same phylogenetic genus, such as golden-winged warblers and blue-winged warblers. It's pretty obvious why. For sparks to fly between bird species, they must be similar in size and conversant in each other's mating calls and rituals. In the case of your local love birds, robins and mockingbirds are not in the same genus, or even in the same family, the next classification grouping. And though mockingbirds, as their name suggests, may be able to mimic a robin's mating call, robins are typically 1½ times as heavy, making it unlikely that these two could make, well, a good fit. Therefore, says Patrick Burns, director of the Population and Habitat Program at the National Audubon Society, you've either witnessed some "seriously confused" creatures or overindulged in the electric Kool-Aid.

(Contributed by Stephanie Pearson)

Q: Why do we still see caterpillars in the fall? Shouldn't they be butterflies by now?

—*Nancy Lynn Cole, Green Bay, Wisconsin*

A: Most species of moths and butterflies—a.k.a. Lepidoptera—hatch in late spring, crawl about as caterpillars all summer, pupate in fall and winter (they're called cocoons if they're moths, chrysalises if they're butterflies), and emerge as adults the next spring. But there are caterpillars that roam the Earth year-round, with each of the 112,000 species following its own savvy DNA-programmed schedule. According to University of Illinois entomologist Philip Nixon, lepidopterans are highly adaptive creatures that have evolved to take precise advantage of conditions like weather and the waxing and waning of their host plants. Consider the Isabella tiger moth, seen from coast to coast. In late summer, its eggs hatch into woolly bear caterpillars, which spend the fall munching lamb's-quarters and other plants. In the winter, when food is scarce, the fuzzy fellas hibernate, only to cocoon in the spring and emerge in early summer as adults. The complexities go on. Some moths produce multiple generations in a year, so you might see their offspring at any time. An example is the magnificent monarch; its caterpillars eat only milkweed, the pursuit of which (along with cold temperatures) spurs the butterflies to make their annual 3,000-mile migrations up and down our continent.

Q: Why are other primates so much stronger than us?

—*JIM WELLS, CHICAGO, ILLINOIS*

A: You must be talking about the great apes—gorillas, orangutans, and chimpanzees. On a pound-for-pound basis, apes do have more muscle than humans, says Adrienne Zihlman, an anthropologist at the University of California at Santa Cruz. Our muscle fibers are virtually identical and can exert the same force per unit of muscle mass, but apes have about 7 percent more muscle tissue per pound of body weight, most of it housed in the upper body. Since apes walk on all fours, they have long, extremely burly arms, which constitute 18 percent of their body weight, compared with 8 or 9 percent for us. Their hands are two to three times heavier, and their bones and torsos more robust. Turning to a more visceral definition—who could kick whose hiney—our more agile cousins don't share the human tendency toward physical inhibition and, if threatened, will grab, hold, bite, and punch with reckless abandon. (That's why it's called "going ape.") If it makes you feel better, our legs are much stronger. So should you ever encounter a hotheaded chimp with his dukes up, just hightail it back the way you came. You're no Tarzan.

Q: I've heard that most poisonous snakes on the planet have mouths that are too small to bite us. What gives?

—*Tim Russell, Seattle, Washington*

A: Swallow your pride, bub. Humans are barely a blip on most poisonous snakes' radar screens. Many of the world's deadliest serpents, for instance, live in remote, unpopulated stretches of the Australian outback. They evolved for millions of years without the threat of marauding sheep ranchers, and thus had no great need to puncture the human epidermis. Consider the irony of elapids, the snake family that includes the western brown, death adder, and black tiger—often described as the world's deadliest reptilian triumvirate. Each snake packs enough neurotoxins to paralyze an adult, but their nickel-size mouths—designed to fit around small lizards or snakes—only open just wide enough to nip (not chomp) a human limb. And their fixed ¼-inch fangs have difficulty penetrating a pair of jeans. Experts are busy debating which snakes are the most poisonous (the ones that kill you quickest, or the ones that kill you deadest), so the question of whether they could even bite you in the first place remains unsettled. But as Penn State–Hazleton biologist J. Brian Hauge warns, "It's very dangerous to assume that the most venomous snakes have mouths too small to do damage to you." Indeed, being wrong would really bite. (*Contributed by Stephanie Pearson*)

Q: Can dolphins and whales breathe through their mouths?

—JAMES B. MOON, STEAMBOAT SPRINGS, COLORADO

A: No, because there's not a direct connection between a cetacean's mouth and its respiratory system. The airways of these mammals run in a straight line from the blowhole—the top-of-the-head opening that allows air to move in and out—to a pair of nasal cavities called nares and on to the larynx, the trachea, and the lungs. Unlike our own piping, this is a closed system, with rare exceptions. San Diego marine veterinarian Sam Ridgway says some cetaceans can relax the sphincter that holds the larynx in place and dislodge it, allowing air to move through the mouth and down the trachea. "It's unusual," he says, "but I have seen playful dolphins disconnect the larynx so they can blow bubbles." This anatomical quirk occurs only in toothed whales—including the sperm whale, narwhal, orca, and porpoise—and it helps explain an old maritime mystery. Back in the days when whalers hunted sperm whales, they often reported seeing fish fly through the air when the leviathans surfaced. We now know what's happening: A fish destined for the whale's gullet can sometimes jar its captor's larynx free and wriggle into the trachea and up the nasal passage. And what would you do if you had a herring in your nostril? Thar she blows!

Q: How far out to sea do I need to get to be safe from mosquitoes?

—*Bernadette Pampuch Rivero, Ragged River, Bahamas*

A: Be prepared to row your boat a long way if you want to escape the proboscis of any of the world's three thousand species of skeeters. Jack Petersen, an entomologist at Florida A&M University who researches mosquito control, says the black salt-marsh mosquito—a critter he calls "Florida's public enemy number one"—is often found 20 miles offshore. Of course, they can't actually smell you from that far away. The maximum distance from which a downwind mosquito can sniff blood, so to speak—by detecting the CO_2 and lactic acid that humans give off—is about 60 yards. Long-distance mosquito travel is more a function of riding wind currents than flying with intent. Ultimately, the question to ask is not where but when. If you go out on the water at midday, when heavier breezes blow toward shore and send the bugs back to their nests, you might need more sunscreen, but you'll greatly reduce the need for DEET.

Q: Is it true that raptors can't release their prey in flight? I've heard stories of ospreys drowning and eagles crashing because they latched onto something too big.

—HANNAH SHEPARD, BRALORNE, BRITISH COLUMBIA, CANADA

A: Sometimes a raptor whose eyes are bigger than its wings will attach itself to prey that's so weighty it's unable to get off the ground. Pat Redig, director of the University of Minnesota's Raptor Center, says this is because the birds have special ratcheting tendons that allow them to grip tightly even when their muscles aren't flexed. The tendons consist of two notched tubes, one inside the other; when the raptor makes a grab, the notches catch—the same action that allows perching birds to hold onto a branch while asleep. Unhitching the tendons requires a quick flex of the muscles—but quick is a relative term when you're an osprey frantically trying to detach from a deceptively big carp. If the raptor can't let go in time to pick up wing speed, a heavy fish or animal can drag it down. Still, when a bird does crash, it's usually not the result of mechanics so much as stubbornness. Redig once took his pet red-tailed hawk out to hunt, and the hawk "captured" a very large rabbit and was clearly determined not to let go. "The rabbit," he recalls, "scurried down a hole, leaving the hawk desperately trying to keep its head above ground." Call it the earth inheriting the not so meek.

Q: Is it OK to take your dog on long runs?

—MILES GAVIN, SAN DIEGO, CALIFORNIA

A: Pretty much every canine loves to run, but according to Jacque Schultz, a dog trainer at the American Society for the Prevention of Cruelty to Animals (ASPCA) headquarters in New York, serious runners should pick their breed carefully. Large dogs, such as retrievers, Dobermans, and Rhodesian Ridgebacks, make great running mates because they've been bred to have long, graceful strides and sturdy joints. Many dogs don't like to run continuously for more than 10 miles, but some hardy breeds—like the Siberian husky— would have no trouble finishing a marathon. Most midsize models are fine for up to 5 miles. Scrappers like the foot-tall Jack Russell terrier can hold their own, too, but dogs smaller than that don't have the legs or the hearts to keep up. Dogs with short snouts, arthritis, or hip dysplasia shouldn't take on long distances, and age is crucial. Puppies don't fully develop until 12 to 18 months, and high-impact exercise can lead to sore joints or bone damage. Beyond that, use common sense: Start slow, opt for dirt trails over pavement, bring water, examine paw pads, and don't run your Saint Bernard in August. In fact, if a pooch ever shows signs of heat distress—excessive panting, very red gums, or lagging behind—head for some shade and get him wet.

Q: Why don't you hear of turkey eggs and why don't we ever eat them?

—DAN DOSMANN, GRANGER, INDIANA

A: Some would argue it's a matter of taste. "As a poor graduate student, I could eat all the turkey eggs I wanted for free, because unused eggs were thrown out of the lab," chuckles USDA research physiologist John Proudman, of his days studying the bird's reproductive productivity at the University of Wisconsin at Madison. Despite this cheap and easy protein source, Proudman says he declined to make the dishwater-colored, rust-spotted, fist-size orbs a dietary staple: "Turkey eggs are tough and chewy." Proudman's former mentor at Madison, professor of avian physiology Bernard Wentworth, disagrees. He eats the U. of W. surplus ova twice a week, scrambled. "Sure, the membrane is tougher," he concedes, adding that he has to whack them hard on the counter to break the shell, "but once you get to the contents, I don't think anyone could tell them apart from chicken eggs." Whatever the case, it's a moot point for producers, since turkey eggs cost anywhere from $0.75 to $1 a pop. That's because turkeys mature slowly, lay only 90 to 100 eggs every 25 weeks (versus up to 280 from chickens), and devour twice as much grain. (*Contributed by Stephanie Pearson*)

Q: What does it mean when a squirrel chatters at me?

—MARIA RICAPITO, BROOKLYN, NEW YORK

A: This long multisyllabic call means different things for different squirrels. First there's the ground squirrel; females of this variety live in close-knit groups, or "coteries," while the males are always off doing their own thing. As Cornell University animal behaviorist Paul Sherman explains, when a slow-moving predator (like you) seems to be posing a threat, one of the females starts chattering as a heads-up to the others. In some cases, he says, this represents a "selfless act of nepotism," in that the chatterer, by becoming the center of attention, gives its life to allow its kin to escape. Then there's the individualistic tree squirrel; for these rodents, the chatter seems to be a way of telling a large animal, "I see you, so don't waste your time trying to catch me." The noise is just one of several barks, squeals, and cries in a squirrel's vocabulary; others connote "I'm angry," "Time to come home, Junior," and "I've just mated with her; keep your mitts off." When a squirrel spots a truly scary predator, like a hawk, it emits a high-pitched shriek. For ground squirrels, this creates pandemonium, as the critters all start squeaking and scrambling for cover. The more aggressive tree squirrel hopes it will dissuade the hunter from attacking. When this doesn't work, he tries that old standby, running.

Q: When a spider builds a web from tree to tree, how does it string the initial thread across such a wide distance?

—JAMES B. MOON, OAK CREEK, COLORADO

A: It doesn't take much legwork. All the arachnid has to do is release an ultralight silk strand—one of seven varieties the average web-building North American temperate forest spider manufactures in its abdominal silk glands—and the wind, which can carry the fine thread up to 6 feet away, does the rest. Electrostatic forces (the same ones that stick balloons to TVs) or a simple, breeze-induced tangle affixes the thread to a tree branch, blade of grass, flower stem, or whatever else it happens upon. After this nearly invisible temporary line is set, the spider uses it as scaffolding to walk along and unspool what entomologists call the "bridge thread," the first structurally solid span, upon which the rest of the web will hang. It then walks back on the bridge thread while cutting the initial thread with its fangs and tidying it up into a ball that will eventually be consumed and recycled for future tightrope jaunts. Finally, the enterprising spider puts up the web's circumference, attaches spoke-like radii, and erects the trademark sticky spirals—the snare's deadly vortex. All done in roughly 40 minutes, start to finish.

(Contributed by Stephanie Pearson)

Why do flies need compound eyes?

—*Shirley Beck, Olympia, Washington*

A: Like all insects, flies have compound eyes made up of numerous facets, or ommatidia. Houseflies have about 350 facets per eye, while dragonflies have a whopping 30,000. According to John Meyer, an entomology professor at North Carolina State University, each ommatidium feeds the brain data about its own segment of the field of vision, producing an image like a pixel on your computer screen, and these form a mosaic in the fly's brain. This information—essentially describing light and color—is fairly limited compared with what the human eye takes in, so insects have poor long-distance vision. But their compound eyes provide two important advantages. First, they allow the fly to detect movement much faster than we can, because their flicker fusion rate—the speed at which the eyes can fuse separate images into a continuous "movie"—is five times greater than ours. This is why flies can elude capture and zoom at insane speeds without crashing. Second, since compound eyes are spherical, flies can see what's behind them. So no matter how stealthily you sneak up on the buggers, they see you coming every time.

Q: **When you throw chum into the ocean to attract sharks, how fast does the "scent" travel through the water?**

—GARY JENKINS, AURORA, COLORADO

A: The answer, compliments of Jeff Graham, executive director of the Birch Aquarium, at the Scripps Institution of Oceanography, in San Diego, sounds like a Chinese proverb: "The scent chemicals reach the shark when the current delivers them there." So charting the chum's spread is about as easy as measuring the speed and direction of the current. Dropped into a 3-knot current off the coast of South Africa, for example, the blood and tiny fish particles that a shark "smells" travel just around that fast. "The chum is what we call a point source," Graham says, "like a smokestack at a factory. If you're downwind of it, you'll be in the cone-shaped 'corridor' where the scent particles are. If not, then you won't even know it's there." A shark can follow this bloody trail for a mile or more, thanks to its olfactory groove, a U-shaped slit inside its mouth. This hypersensitive nose of sorts can sniff out one part blood in 1.5 million parts seawater (that's one tiny molecule per 25 gallons of water). The shark then tracks the "scent" to its source—or anything delectable, human or otherwise, that happens to be floating in its path.

Q: Can an African elephant and an Asian elephant mate?

—LENARD MILICH, BALI, INDONESIA

A: Different species can sometimes produce offspring together, as in the case of a mule, the sexually sterile creation of a horse and a donkey. It's much more difficult for the African elephant (*Loxodonta african*) and the Asian elephant (*Elephas maximus*), which are not just different species but different genera. As Lori Eggert, a conservation geneticist at the Smithsonian's National Museum of Natural History, explains, these two heavyweights, which separated 5 million years ago, still share the same number of chromosomes, 56, so the math works out. But with important genes in different places, it's a "less than perfect match." Case in point: Motty, a male hybrid born in 1978 at the Chester Zoo, in Chester, England. The only known crossover elephant, Motty died after 12 days, succumbing to an intestinal infection that may or may not have been caused by bad genes.

* * * * * * * *

Q: When a fly wants to land on the ceiling, does it do a half roll or a half loop?

—BUDDY BROWN, LUBBOCK, TEXAS

A: Neither. For a long time, people believed that the common housefly, *Musca domestica*, performed a stunt pilot's half-barrel roll when approaching the ceiling. But in 1958,

LIFE... NOTHING BUT LIFE

freeze-frame photography revealed that something else was going on. As Caltech insect physiologist Michael Dickinson explains, first the bug-eyed fella flies right side up at a low angle and in a direct line toward the upper deck. Just prior to impact, it instinctively extends its forelegs over its head and grabs the ceiling, using hooks or sticky pads at the ends of its legs. With the fly's front feet firmly grounded, momentum swings the lower half of its body up, like a trapeze artist. Spider-Man's got nothing on Superfly.

·   ·   ·   ·   ·   ·   ·   ·

Q: You often hear about lost animals, including dogs and cats, traveling extraordinary distances to find their way home. Is there any truth to this?

—CRAIG COLLINS, SANTA ROSA, CALIFORNIA

A: According to Bonnie Beaver, a professor of small-animal medicine at Texas A&M University, the vast majority of these Disneyesque stories "turn out to be either hoaxes or cases of mistaken identity in which an overly hopeful owner mistakes a similar animal for the real McCoy." As for the handful of verified cases, animals have a good basic sense of direction and might be capable of wandering in the general direction of home until they eventually stumble on familiar sights, sounds, and scents—the latter of which dogs can detect from at least 5 miles away. "Picture your house at the middle of several concentric circles with your dog at the

outer edge," Beaver says. "Each ring represents a different
smell that the dog is familiar with. No matter how many
wrong turns it makes, it's going to eventually find its way
home." Scientists suspect that more impressive feats of navigation, such as migrations or uncanny "incredible jour-
neys," would require a sort of biological compass—one that
has been found only in birds and fish. The topic clearly
needs more scientific elbow grease. Who do we call to get
funding for a re-creation of *Lassie Come Home?*

•   •   •   •   •   •   •   •

**Q: My friend told me that giraffes can't make
a sound because they don't have vocal
cords. How sad! Is this true?**

—NANCY JONES, LONG BRANCH, NEW JERSEY

A: Breathe easy. Giraffes do have a set of vocal chords,
a.k.a. a larynx. But they're unable to emit more than a low
moo or wheeze, so the 18-foot-tall watchtowers of the

savanna communicate instead by making the air in their 8-foot-long necks vibrate. "It's called Helmholtz resonance," says Elizabeth von Muggenthaler, a biologist who recently completed a three-and-a-half-year study of giraffe bioaccoustics at zoos in North and South Carolina. "It's kind of the same principle as when you blow air across the top of a Coke bottle: Air circulates inside the bottle and is then released through the top." Von Muggenthaler has identified two distinct head movements that, she believes, may create Helmholtz resonance. In a "neck stretch," the giraffe swings its head to its rear, and then rapidly sweeps it up and forward like a serpent; in the second, a "head throw," the giraffe lowers its chin and then quickly raises it skyward. In both cases, the calls produced are mostly infrasonic, too low in pitch to be heard by humans but apparently audible to calves and the giraffe's mate—even through stands of baobab trees and herds of safari-goers.

●　　●　　●　　●　　●　　●　　●　　●

Q: Why aren't there fireflies on the West Coast?

—JAMES BECKER, PORTLAND, OREGON

A: To be precise, about 30 of North America's 200 or so species of firefly live on the West Coast. Surprisingly, only one of those species—the landlubbing glowworm—actually glows. Scientists define a firefly as any insect belonging to the family Lampyridae (*lam-PIER-ri-dee*), which are slender, soft-bodied beetles usually between 4.5 and 20 millimeters long, with mostly concealed heads. In other words, a bug doesn't have to be bioluminescent to be a firefly. Go figure. According to James Lloyd, an entomologist at the University of Florida–Gainesville, scientists know a lot about lightning bugs—for instance, that they light up in order to attract mates and, on occasion, to startle predators—but he's not aware of any rigorous studies on why *Photinus pyralis*, the most common six-legged light bulb in the U.S., isn't found west of the Rockies. A widely proposed theory, says Lloyd, is that the snails, slugs, and worms that make up *P. pyralis*'s preferred diet live only in the East; however, he adds that other factors, like humidity levels and soil types, may also be significant. Or it could simply be that non-flashy species already fill the western biological niche in which *P. pyralis* would thrive. Until some researcher as curious as Mr. Becker tackles the problem—he is currently too busy naming several dozen new species to do it himself— Lloyd's guess is the best answer. "The wheels of science turn slow," he admits.

Q: What do mosquitoes eat when people or other warm-blooded animals aren't around?

—DAVE WYANT, PHOENIX, ARIZONA

A: Your first mistake is assuming that all mosquitoes bite people or other warm-blooded animals. Fact is, a large number of the world's roughly 2,000 mosquito species prefer birds, while others dine on cold-blooded critters, such as frogs, and wouldn't touch human or horse for a million bucks. Your second mistake (a common one) is assuming that blood is a mosquito's only food source. Actually, they eat good old-fashioned carbohydrates, those found in fresh fruits, succulent grasses, and the nectar of flowers. So why on earth do mosquitoes bite animals? Females need the protein and amino acids found in blood in order to form their eggs, explains Wayne Crans, director of the Mosquito Research and Control Unit at Rutgers University. "If the females don't succeed," explains Crans, "they don't have babies." Males have no need for blood, so they don't bite people. After finding a mate and fertilizing her eggs, they bite the dust at the not-so-ripe age of four days.

Q: How many calories would a hummingbird need to consume in a day if it were the size of a human?

—*Mark McCubbin, Madison, Wisconsin*

A: The diminutive birds John James Audubon described as "glittering fragments of the rainbow" have a faster metabolism than any other vertebrate on Earth. The reason, says Robert Dudley, a professor of integrated biology at the University of Texas at Austin who specializes in all things hummingbird, is that unlike most birds, which flap their wings vertically to keep aloft, hummingbirds beat their wings nearly horizontally—roughly 53 times per second—as though they were treading water. This allows them to hover in place like helicopters when, say, feeding on sugar water outside your window. Of course, such hyperactivity takes its toll. An average ruby-throated hummingbird—the common East Coast variety—weighs just 4 grams but burns around 3½ calories per day. Just to stay alive, says Dudley, it must find thousands of flowers and drink approximately its body weight in nectar each day. Computing the calories required per gram of weight, you'd find that a man-size hummingbird of 180 pounds would need to scrounge up around 82,000 calories every 24 hours—the equivalent of 228 chocolate milk shakes. God save us all from the day when humongous hummingbirds descend on our diners in search of vital carbs. "It wouldn't be pretty," warns Dudley. "It just might get downright ugly."

Q: Why do hammerhead sharks have such strange-shaped heads?

—Eric Waters, North Vancouver, British Columbia, Canada

A: "Good question," says Kim Holland, a professor at the Hawaii Institute of Marine Biology outside Honolulu. "I just had a student earn his Ph.D. on this very subject." For starters, he explains, the wide head acts "like a canard," providing lift and making the shark a more agile swimmer (bad news for the speedy squid, one of its favorite snacks). The hammer-shaped mug also enriches the shark's sensory system. Its two nostrils occupy prime real estate on the front corners of the broad head, where they're spaced far enough apart to detect changes in the concentration of a scent from one side to the other. This makes the shark an olfactory all-star, able to home in on its prey. But perhaps the most important function of the odd-shaped noggin, says Holland, is the added surface area it provides for the hammerhead's ampullae of Lorenzini, the extremely sensitive jelly-filled electrore-ceptors located around its mouth. Scientists believe these sensor cells act like metal detectors. They pick up weak electric fields, emitted by all living organisms, and then relay the signals to the shark's central nervous system to alert the dorsal-finned demon to prey cam-ouflaged on the ocean floor. Which is *really* bad news for bottom-dwelling stingrays, another hammerhead staple.

The Bottle Head

The Hammer Head

The Flat Head

The Saw Head

Q: What's the fastest insect?

—ELLIE KUNKEL, SAVAGE, MINNESOTA

A: Given the vagaries of wind speed and the fact that insects zig and zag, it's very hard to measure the swiftness of flying bugs. But there's someone on the case: entomology professor Thomas Walker, who, with his students at the University of Florida, undertook a massive study of bug trivia for the online *Book of Insect Records.* On the subject of flight speed, they turned to the most exhaustive research to date, that of T. J. Dean, a physics postgrad at the Australian Defence Force Academy. Dean's 2003 report, which drew upon reams of peer-reviewed studies, found that the "highest reliably measured airspeeds," free of wind influence, belong to the desert locust (the ones that plague the Old Testament), which moves at 21 miles per hour—about as fast as an Olympic sprinter. But there may yet be an undocumented speed king out there: Many have odds on the Australian dragonfly, but so far it's eluded the radar gun.

. . . .

Q: What is the smallest dinosaur ever found?

—JERRI CALLANTINE, OGDEN, UTAH

A: From 1859 until recently, the 3-foot-long, Jurassic-period *Compsognathus longipes,* a fleet-footed lizard eater, held the title. But a recent find has bumped *Compsognathus* off its itty-bitty throne. According to University of Maryland paleontologist Thomas Holtz, *Microraptor zhaoianus*, unearthed in China's Liaoning Province in the late 1990s, is now the smallest of the giants. Micro, which measured about 16 inches from snout to toe, resembled its relative the velociraptor, but with a few avian extras: It lived in trees and had a special toe for grasping branches. Why did it evolve to be so shrimpy? While its Cretaceous-period cousins were chowing on larger prey, the small-mammal population skyrocketed. There was a niche to be filled, and Micro stepped up to the plate.

Q: Why do so many different animals have tails?

—*GEOFF WITT, HICKORY, NORTH CAROLINA*

A: "The better question," says Philip Johns, an assistant professor of biology at Swarthmore College, in Pennsylvania, "is, Why do so many animals *not* have tails? They're incredibly useful." Defined as any extension of the backbone beyond the trunk, tails first appeared several hundred million years ago as propulsion devices on the chordate ancestors of hagfish, eel-like swimmers living up to 16,000 feet below sea level. Over time, as fish evolved into amphibians and took to dry land, tails became pretty useless for propulsion, but the appendages remain nearly ubiquitous today because of myriad uses that developed through natural selection. New World monkeys, for example, have prehensile tails that let them swing among branches. Squirrels use the appendage for balance. Dogs' tails help them communicate (we all know wagging means happiness). And some lizards are blessed with detachable models: When nabbed by their tail, they simply release it and slither off from predators unharmed.

. . . .

Q: A keen-eyed human sees 20/20. By that measure, how well can eagles see?

—*Robert Selzer, New Haven, Connecticut*

A: If you could ask very nicely and get a bald eagle to sit in front of an eye chart, his score would probably be about 20/8, two and a half times better than a human's. Such is the visual acuity of the wedge-tailed eagle, which scientists have tested; in real terms, it means a small object we can spot from 10 feet away can be detected by this bird from 25 feet. Eagles' sharp eyesight comes partly from optic lobes and eyeballs that are, in relative terms, significantly bigger than a mammal's, says Graham Martin, professor of avian

LIFE... NOTHING BUT LIFE

sensory sciences at England's University of Birmingham. Their larger peepers also contain much more densely packed cones in the fovea, the area in the retina that sharpens images—picture a high-end camera using finer-grain film. To top it off, you and I have only one fovea in each eye, and an eagle has two. No wonder they look so proud.

*   *   *   *   *   *   *   *

Q: Why does tomato juice de-skunk my dog, whereas my guava-strawberry shampoo doesn't help at all?

—GILLIAN ASHLEY, GARDINER, MAINE

A: We'll give Ms. Ashley an A for aggressive trial and error, but the bad news is, her entire premise is flawed: Even tomato juice doesn't work as a skunk-spray deodorizer. Giving Fido a V-8 bath is no better than soaking Pepe Le Pew in $5 perfume—it will temporarily cover up the skunk's stinky calling card but do nothing to combat the source. To really quell the smell, says William Wood, a chemistry professor at California's Humboldt State University, try his mad scientist's blend of 1 quart hydrogen peroxide (the common 3 percent variety), ¼ cup baking soda, and a teaspoon of liquid laundry detergent. This concoction will blitzkrieg the malodorous thiols—the skunk's offending chemical compounds, which contain rotten-egg-smelling sulfur—and through oxidation transform them into odorless sulfonic acids. Douse a sprayed dog with this recipe, rinse, and repeat until the odor disappears. It's harmless, but beware: Hydrogen peroxide has one side effect long embraced by midwestern mallrats and SoCal surfers alike. "It's strong stuff," warns Wood. "It can turn a black Lab into a chocolate Lab."

* * * * * * * *

Q: If humans evolved from apes, why do we still have apes?

—TOM ADAIR, MINNEAPOLIS, MINNESOTA

A: Um, to throw things at us when we visit the zoo? Seriously, though, "evolution produces a pattern like a tree with many branches," says Marian Dagosto, a biologist at Northwestern University, in Evanston, Illinois. In other words, she says, "The best way to view the evolutionary relationship between a chimpanzee and a human is not that humans evolved from chimps, but that humans and chimpanzees share a common ancestor." In the Miocene epoch, which extended from about 23 million to 5 million years ago, there were untold numbers of ape species. Scientists believe that one of these unnamed species evolved into *Homo sapiens* about 300,000 years ago. The remaining apes either went extinct or evolved into one of the four species that exist today: the chimpanzee, gorilla, orangutan, and bonobo. "According to fossil records," adds Dagosto, "that Miocene ancestor probably looked more like a chimpanzee than a human." That explains why, in the family album, your great-great-grandmother might look a little hairy.

Q: I picked up a spider and it screamed at me—I swear! Is this possible?

—JAN BRETT, DORSET, ENGLAND

A: If you have good ears, you might have heard a stridulation. That's the noise a spider makes when it's courting a mate or trying to ward off predators, and it's produced by rubbing a scraper-like organ against a file-like organ—as a cricket does, but far less noisy. University of California–Berkeley arachnologist Eileen Hebets says most spiders stridulate too quietly for humans to hear; an exception is Australia's barking spider, a kind of tarantula that lets out a hissing sound when threatened. It's a far cry from a scream, though. Truth is, spiders have no eardrums, and only "hear" one another through vibrations. The spined micrathena, common in the U.S., vibrates with such gusto that if you picked one up, you'd think it was a wind-up toy. All in all, spiders are silent types. "When I dream, I almost always dream about spiders," Hebets says. "But rarely can I hear them in my sleep."

* * * * * * * *

Q: Do animals have orgasms?

—AMY PETERSEN, BEND, OREGON

A: There's been more research on this topic than you might care to know about, and the answer is yes—at least for primates. According to Marlene Zuk, a professor of biology at the University of California at Riverside and author of *Sexual*

Selections: What We Can and Can't Learn About Sex from Animals, studies of macaques and bonobos reveal that both males and females have orgasms, measured as contractions of muscles and tissues in their nether regions. What has scientists scratching their heads is that almost all of the observed orgasms among females have occurred not during copulation but in homosexual encounters or masturbation. It gets more mysterious when we look at the rest of the mammal world, but some speculate that, based on informal study of rabbits, dogs, and other critters, the orgasm phenomenon is universal. One ferret researcher, for example, insisted his female subjects climax— judging merely by the looks on their faces.

●　　●　　●　　●　　●　　●　　●　　●

Q: Mountain goats clearly are terrific climbers, but do they ever fall and hurt themselves?

—SCOTT ANDERSON, PORTLAND, OREGON

A: "They sure do," says Gayle Joslin, a wildlife biologist with Montana's Department of Fish, Wildlife & Parks. "You'll find their carcasses at the bottoms of avalanche chutes or see live ones with their horns facing the wrong way, an indication of a fall." But it doesn't happen often. Mountain goats (which, despite their name, are more closely related to African antelopes than to the domestic

LIFE... NOTHING BUT LIFE

goat) have low centers of gravity, strong calf muscles, and extremely deft feet. Their hooves have two parts—a soft bottom pad and a hard shell surrounding it—that enable them to nimbly grip both rough and smooth surfaces in their mountainous habitat, which ranges from Alaska to New Mexico. And consider that when one of these rock jocks is seriously hurt, it's often as the result of waging a turf battle or dodging an aerial attack from a golden eagle—a predator of their young—on vertiginous slopes that would make the most seasoned climbers' toes curl. "The amazing thing," says Joslin, "is how *infrequently* they fall."

* * * * * * * *

Q: From how high up can a flying squirrel safely launch?

—JAN NESSET, DURANGO, COLORADO

A: As you probably know, flying squirrels—a subfamily of 43 species found in North America, Europe, and Asia—don't really fly. They glide, by taking off from a high perch, spreading a special membrane called a patagium, which resembles a bat wing, and soaring up to 150 feet to another tree. A split second before impact, they slam on the brakes by changing shape from that of a sleek F-16 to a bell-shaped parachute. John Scheibe, a biology professor at Southeast Missouri State University, says that because flying squirrels are so light—about two ounces, whereas gray tree squirrels can reach a pound—their only "flight" limitation is the height of the tree. (Thankfully, nobody's tried launching them from airplanes.) But in theory, if you discounted atmospheric obstacles, a flying squirrel leaping from a 30,000-foot tree could make it down to earth in 45 minutes and expend only one-tenth of its daily metabolic output. For this Iron Squirrel event, it had better bring some nuts.

• • • • • • • • •

Q: Why do cows have four teats? They only rarely give birth to twins, much less quads.

—SARAH KAST, MINNEAPOLIS, MINNESOTA

A: You're right: Cows generally bear only one calf per pregnancy, so it does seem odd that they'd have so many teats. But according to Professor Walter Hurley of the University of Illinois, we're pretty sure that the cow's remote ancestors had more than one baby—maybe many more—and that, like most animals, they've evolved toward fewer offspring. Fossil records show that millions of years ago, cows and pigs shared a common ancestor, an animal that looked more pig than cow. It probably had multiple offspring, like a pig, which has litters of 12 to 14, so it would have needed more teats to nurse them. It seems the modern cow retained those extra teats, which isn't a bad thing. Extra nipples means there will always be a supply of milk should one teat get infected and stop working. Interestingly, 50 percent of dairy calves are born with *more than* four teats; the mostly useless "supernumerary" nipples can occur even in humans.

LIFE... NOTHING BUT LIFE

Q: When birds swoop around en masse, how do they decide who does the steering?

—VIRGINIA GRABOW, TIGARD, OREGON

A: You've opened a big can of worms, and we don't mean the kind that our flying friends like to feast on. While many animal groups—packs of wolves, for example—travel under the guidance of a dominant leader, it appears that with large flocks of birds, such as those two hundred starlings you might see carousing around your neighborhood, there is no leader of the pack. So what's going on? That's what California computer scientist Craig Reynolds wanted to know. "I used to go out in my backyard and watch the flocks and wonder how in the world they worked," he says. So in 1986 he set out to crack the case by creating a virtual-bird program that he dubbed Boids. Reynolds theorized that all birds follow a few specific rules, such as trying to fly as close together as possible without colliding and trying to maintain the same speed and direction. When he programmed the computer to reflect these rules and hit return, sure enough, the digital birds coalesced and flew in unison. He found that the "boid" out in front might lead the flock in one direction but then initiate a change that would result in another boid becoming the momentary "leader," with no single member doing all the steering.

Ornithologists haven't proven that Reynolds's program precisely mirrors flocking behavior, but his is the prevailing theory for explaining this "emergent system"—a term chaos theorists use to describe a system in which order emerges from the behavior of simple parts. Sounds like something Congress should look into.

●   ●   ●   ●   ●   ●   ●

Q: If a fly gets trapped in my car and I drive 50 miles, what happens to it when it escapes?

—NELL GHARIBIAN, BOSTON, MASSACHUSETTS

A: This is a case where being less socially advanced is a good thing. A honeybee can't find its way home from more than a mile away, and it would be rejected by hives in a new territory and die within days. Houseflies, which don't form the same complex social structures as bees, would stay on their new turf and get along just fine. According to Lee Townsend, an entomologist at the University of Kentucky, a fly would simply follow its nose around in pursuit of the rotting organic matter that it lives on. Its only contact might

LIFE... NOTHING BUT LIFE

be with the other flies at a popular dung pile, where, picking up chemical signals put out by the opposite sex, it could find a mate. The pair's relationship would be brief—flies don't waste time on courtship—and then the male, for the remainder of its two-week life span, would head off in search of more gooey dead stuff. If you're a fly, how could you ask for anything more?

.   .   .   .

Q: Do pigs really kill more people than sharks?

—*ANONYMOUS*

A: Could be, says Ricky Langley, of the North Carolina Department of Health and Human Services. Without even addressing quagmires like disease and pollution, Langley says that, in a typical year, the barnyard hog is probably responsible for slightly more fatalities. The numbers reveal that swine cause about 0.96 deaths per year through "direct animal events" (like knocking their keepers down and trampling them), beating out the overrated shark, at 0.73, and demonstrating that the wild places aren't as scary as your average farm. Cattle, for instance, fatally gore and crush 24 people a year, and about 88 people are thrown from horses and killed. But if you truly fear death by animal, toss out the car keys: Deer kill about 14 Americans per month, mostly through collisions with front bumpers.

Q: Is the phrase "drink like a fish" a misnomer?

—GUILLERMO ENRIQUEZ, TEMPE, ARIZONA

A: That depends on your definition of "drink." As Professor Richard Strange, of the University of Tennessee's Department of Forestry, Wildlife and Fisheries, explains, a fish's hydration depends chiefly on osmosis, which occurs whenever the concentration of salt in the water is lower on one side of a semipermeable membrane than on the other. In fish, this fluid exchange happens mostly through cell walls in the gills. Saltwater fish, poor things, have an unquenchable thirst, because they are constantly being dehydrated by the saltier sea all around them. Thus, their lives depend on the additional water content in the critters they eat, and the water they gulp down with them. (Most of the salt is filtered out in the kidneys.) Freshwater fish, being saltier than their environment, absorb water like a sponge, so they never have to "drink"—on the contrary, they urinate almost constantly. Which might explain those warm spots in the lake.

. . . .

Q: How did elephants get trunks?

—ASA TAPLEY, WASHINGTON, D.C.

A: Since a trunk doesn't contain bones, it doesn't leave behind fossils, and without fossils, paleontologists have to get creative about studying the trunk's evolution. By tracing changes in two cavities on the front of the skull, they've found what they think is the granddaddy of all elephants, a dog-size creature called *Phosphatherium escuilliei,* which lived 55 million years ago. But this tapir-like animal seems to have been trunkless. So what happened? Natural selection. As Hezy Shoshani, a biology professor at Eritrea's University of Asmara, explains, most scientists believe that elephants are a product of Cope's Law, which states that most species get bigger as they evolve. Over time, as elephants grew away from the ground, they had a harder time reaching down to get their food. So the trunk was born— probably morphing out of the lip and nose—and soon the big guys had the ultimate browsing tool.

●　　●　　●　　●　　●　　●　　●　　●

Q: What creature can consume the most food in one day, relative to its own weight?

—*MIKE FOUNTOULAKIS, PLANO, TEXAS*

A: Although Japanese world champion hot-dog eater Takeru Kobayashi can eat up to 6 percent of his own weight in wieners, that's put to shame by many beings higher up the gluttony scale. The spotted hyena (more a hunter than a scavenger) can wolf down one-third its own body weight, even the hooves and bones, while two other voracious mammals—the tiny masked shrew and the vampire bat—can gobble and slurp (respectively) a full 100 percent of their weight in 24 hours. Scarier yet, some deep-sea-dwelling, sci-fi-looking breeds of anglerfish, which attract prey by dangling a bioluminescent lure from their foremost dorsal spine, can take down fish their own size in a single gulp. Still, these daunting fuel capacities are eclipsed by some caterpillars. During its final growth stage, the constantly feeding larva of a monarch butterfly consumes an amazing 2.25 times its own weight in milkweed per day. Eat your heart out, Kobayashi.

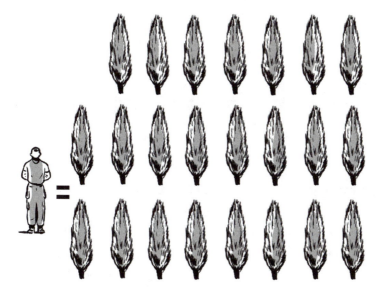

Q: How many trees does it take to supply enough oxygen for one person to survive?

—STEVE YATES, SUGAR LAND, TEXAS

A: First you need to figure how much oxygen one person consumes. Southern Oregon University biology professor John Roden estimates that the average human requires about 130,000 liters per year. Trees both produce and consume O_2, but in a productive tropical rainforest, the average tree releases a net 273,000 liters of oxygen per year. At the other extreme, a desert juniper produces only 6,000 liters or so. So you'd need 21 junipers to keep one human aerated, while a single rainforest specimen produces enough oxygen for two. Next time you see a tree, take a deep breath and say thanks.

•   •   •   •   •   •   •   •   •

Q: Which spider makes the strongest web?

—BRANDON CULBERSON, RALEIGH, NORTH CAROLINA

A: Sadly, no one has volleyed objects into the webs of the 37,000 known spider species to find this out, but when it comes to spinning strong silk, the golden orb weaver (*Nephila clavipes*) is thought to be the champ. According to Cheryl Hayashi, a biology professor at the University of California at Riverside, the female *Nephila*, whose 3-foot webs are found in the Americas as far north as the Carolinas, produces dragline silk that's better at absorbing impact than steel and Kevlar—which explains why its use has been considered for the manufacture of bulletproof vests. The main obstacle: There's no efficient way to corral the cannibalistic spiders en masse, like silkworms, for the sake of extracting their precious superstring.

Q: Why are some animals color-blind?

—*Jordan Paul, Simsbury, Connecticut*

A: With the exception of a few weird sea creatures and nocturnal species, no animal is truly color-blind, but some don't see as many colors as we do. The difference is in the eyes' cones, neuroreceptors that pick up information from different wavelengths of light. The majority of mammals have only two kinds of cones, while most primates, including humans, have three. Why are some critters short-changed? According to Jay Neitz, a professor of cell biology and ophthalmology at the Medical College of Wisconsin, in Milwaukee, when primitive mammals began to flourish, about 100 million years ago, they had four kinds of cones. But because dinosaurs ruled the daytime, these proto-mammals had to skulk after dark, when color is less important, so over time they lost the two types they weren't using; only later did primates evolve a third cone type. Meanwhile, most fish, birds, and reptiles still have four kinds of cones, and some butterflies, like the Japanese yellow swallowtail, have five. Compared with them, we're the ones who are color-blind.

Q: Which animal makes the shortest migration?

—NED BALBO, BALTIMORE, MARYLAND

A: Migration can mean many things, and one scientist's definition might not jibe with another's. Some would call daily movements to and fro a form of migration; by this standard, the short-distance champ might be *Convoluta roscoffensis*, a species of marine flatworm that lives between grains of beach sand. These creatures migrate to the surface at low tide and burrow back down at high tide—a round-trip of less than 8 inches. Then there are vertical migrations, as with Dall sheep, which might descend just a few hundred feet for the winter. But if you mean seasonal migration from one area to another, there are several you'd hardly notice. Many amphibians, like the Yosemite toad, travel less than a quarter mile each spring, from meadows to the pools where they breed. Yet even this outdoes the lowly spotted salamander, whose annual pilgrimage takes it between 100 and 1,000 feet—still, that's a trek for a salamander.

. . . .

Q: Do whales shiver?

—JIM WELLS, CHICAGO, ILLINOIS

A: The shivering mechanism is an involuntary heat-producing tremble seen in most mammals, but it's never been observed in whales. According to John Heyning, a marine biologist at the Natural History Museum of Los Angeles County, that's probably because whales don't need to shiver—their superefficient thermoregulation systems keep their body temperatures steady whether they're off the coast of Hawaii or in 30-degree Arctic water. The big guys' main defense, of course, is the subdermal layer of fatty tissue called blubber, which in a bowhead whale can be 20 inches thick. Leviathans also can shut off blood flow to their fins and flukes if they need to preserve core body heat, thanks to uniquely designed heat-regulating blood vessels. So if you ever do see a whale shiver, beware: The ghost of Ahab may be about.

* * * * * * * *

Q: Where do ants go in the winter?

—PHIN HANSON, MADISON, WISCONSIN

A: Most of the world's 8,000 ant species live in hot climates, but those dwelling in cooler zones spend the winter in nests below or above ground, and their metabolism slows drastically. Where frosts are infrequent, ants typically build quarters above the dirt—as

with weaver ants, which crash in "carton nests" of their own making. Residents of colder latitudes escape the freeze by cozying up in their often elaborate subterranean dens. Wood ants, for instance, like to stay near the surface by day—the entrance mound works as a solar collector—and descend below the frost line at night, as far as 10 feet down. According to Joan M. Herbers, an ecology and biology professor at Ohio State University, there's only one known cold-climate ant that stays above ground: the 2-millimeter acorn ant. Colonies of 30 to 100 of these tiny fellas huddle inside small acorns or hollow sticks, where they stay put throughout the winter—if they didn't, larger ants might come along and poach their crib. "Since possession is nine-tenths of the law," says Herbers, "they're able to keep their homes in the face of intense competition."

· · · · · · · ·

Q: Can any animal kill you without touching you?

—BERNADETTE P. RIVERO, WEST HOLLYWOOD, CALIFORNIA

A: In theory. In the Amazon, for example, you could run into an angry mob of electric eels, which can discharge up to 600 volts into the water, enough to stop a weak heart. You could get too close to a sperm whale, which stuns small prey with sonic blasts—it might knock you silly, and then drowning would be a concern. And snakes like the African black-necked spitting cobra, which can blind you with a well-aimed snootful of toxin, could conceivably do you in. But no such freak deaths have been reported. There are, however, two cases of monkeys killing people by throwing things. Both happened in Malaysia, at the hands of macaques who'd been trained to fetch coconuts, but who protested their forced servitude by hurling them instead.

•　　•　　•　　•　　•　　•　　•　　•

Q: Why are parrots such astounding mimics?
—KRIS TROTTER, MIDDLETON, NEW BRUNSWICK, CANADA

A: Parrots, macaws, and cockatoos have proportionally bigger brains than other birds, as well as exceptional hearing, so they're simply better at discerning subtleties in human speech. Their vocal apparatuses and muscular tongues also make them better than other tweeters at producing human-like sounds. What evolutionary benefit do they gain from their chatterbox talents? According to Tim Wright, a zoologist at the Smithsonian National Zoo, in Washington, D.C., parrots' talkative ways are handy in the jungle, where members of flocks tend to get isolated from one another. Wright says parrots have distinct "languages" that help them identify friends and significant others (parrots are monogamous), but they also can mimic other parrots to increase their chances of integrating into new flocks if the need arises. As for their favorite topic, Wright believes it's office politics. "They talk about who's in charge and who are the peons," he says.

Q: Do plants go potty?

—HAYNES WERNER (AGE 4), WEST GLACIER, MONTANA

A: Plants and people work in very different ways, so comparing them is a bad idea—but for an eager sprout like you we'll make an exception. One big difference involves how they take in nutrition. As Gary Watson, a botanist at Chicago's Morton Arboretum, puts it, "Plants build up, and people break down." In other words, humans get their nutrients by gobbling food, with help from a complex digestive system that breaks the grub down into substances the body can use. Plants make their own food, from a dozen basic building blocks that they borrow from their environment. Since people are less discriminating about their intake than plants are, most of what they eat must be disposed of as waste. A plant takes only what it needs to convert carbon dioxide and water into victuals, using energy from the sun, so there is no waste, only extra oxygen plus some sugar water that seeps out of its roots. Even this is put to good use: It's food to the fungi and bacteria in the soil. "I wouldn't call that waste," says Watson. "I'd call it sharing."

. . . .

Q: Why do loons have red eyes?

—SUSANNA WEBER, STEVENS POINT, WISCONSIN

A: We can rule out hangovers, but after that, things get sketchy. Loons, like a dozen other U.S. species, are born with gray eyes that turn red in their second year. It's not clear why, but David Evers, a biologist at the University of Southern Maine, says some theories hold more water than others. Bright colors can help female birds pick out sexier males, but it's size and plumage that count to a loon, not the eyes. More likely is that red eyes filter out the green and blue light that dominates in deep lakes, making the yellow perch that loons prey on stand out better. But that theory's iffy, too: Loons spend their winters in salt water, hunting different-colored fish. It may be that loons have red eyes not because they're useful but because they *used to be* useful—in other words, maybe they're just evolutionary remnants, like your tonsils, whose original function has been lost.

. . . .

Q: If bees take nectar from poisonous plants, will they make poisonous honey?

—DREW CRAVEN, TRAVERSE CITY, MICHIGAN

A: Legend has it that in the first century B.C., Roman troops under the command of Pompey ate a batch of bad honey and were trampled in battle, but modern bee experts wonder whether such a calamity is even possible. According to Jim Cane, an entomologist with the U.S. Department of Agriculture in Logan, Utah, poison honey could result only if all the bees in a particular hive collected nectar from plants that contain alkaloids toxic to humans— such as ragwort, azaleas, and rhododendrons. But in the

LIFE... NOTHING BUT LIFE

buzzing reality of daily life, bees collect from hundreds of types of plants, so whatever toxins they pick up are diluted to the point of harmlessness. Bottom line? Fear not. But if you must worry, take your honey by the tablespoon rather than the bucket.

· · · · · · · · ·

Q: Does anybody keep vampire bats as pets?

—SUSAN SANFORD, COTTONWOOD, ARIZONA

A: If they do, they're breaking the law. Keeping these egg-size mammals—the common vampire bat, *Desmodus rotundus*, and two other, rarer species—as pets is prohibited in the U.S. For one thing, they can give you rabies, but a bigger concern is the economic damage they cause by preying on livestock, like they do in their native Central and South America. Daniel Abram, founder of the New Mexico Bat Research Institute, says that probably doesn't stop a small black market from dabbling in them. But as we know from zoos and universities licensed to care for the creatures, they don't exactly make cuddly companions. For starters, they need fresh blood every day or they'll die. This means their owners either need to live near a slaughterhouse that will supply them with blood, or must own some goats or chickens that the little guys can sink their teeth into every night. Granted, they're cute—if you like the miniature flying Nosferatu look— but wouldn't you be happier with a kitten?

Q: How do woodpeckers avoid brain damage after hitting their heads against trees all day?

—JAN NESSETT, SOMERS, MONTANA

A: "The bottom line," says Walter Bock, a Columbia University professor of evolutionary biology, "is that the force generated when the woodpecker hits the tree does not pass through its braincase." Instead, it travels along the bird's upper jaw—which, like those of other birds, connects below the brain and allows shock to dissipate throughout the entire body as the bird drills for insects or pecks out a nest. Naturally, some of the blow does reverberate back into the cranium, but since the woodpecker brain's surface area is relatively large, the impact is absorbed as a slap, not a punch. And because the avian skull fits tightly around its bird brain—like a bicycle helmet rather than a jar containing a pickled egg (a rough description of the human smart-muscle)—it prevents internal bruising. Every bit of cushioning helps: According to the only relevant study, conducted in 1979 at UCLA's Neuropsychiatric Institute, the acceleration force felt by a common acorn woodpecker measures between 600 and 1,200 Gs—enough that its eyeballs would literally pop out on impact if it didn't blink.

Index

Real Mosquitoes